77-3312

Other Books by Daniel J. Boorstin

The Americans: The Colonial Experience

The Americans: The National Experience

The Landmark History of the American People

The Mysterious Science of the Law

The Lost World of Thomas Jefferson

The Genius of American Politics

America and the Image of Europe

The Image: A Guide to Pseudo-Events in America

An American Primer (Editor)

☆　　☆　　☆

THE DECLINE OF RADICALISM

REFLECTIONS ON AMERICA TODAY

THE
DECLINE
· OF
RADICALISM

☆ ☆ ☆ ☆ ☆ ☆ ☆

REFLECTIONS
ON AMERICA TODAY

DANIEL J. BOORSTIN

RANDOM HOUSE   NEW YORK

First Printing
98765432
Copyright © 1963, 1967, 1968, 1969 by Daniel J. Boorstin

All rights reserved under International and Pan-American
Copyright Conventions. Published in the United States by
Random House, Inc., New York, and simultaneously in Canada
by Random House of Canada Limited, Toronto
Library of Congress Catalog Card Number: 70–85554
Manufactured in the United States of America
by H. Wolff, New York.
Design by Joan Bastone

to the memory of

IDA and J. M. FRANKEL

believers in the meaning of America

"Now the only way to avoid this shipwreck and to provide for our posterity . . . we must be knit together in this work as one man, we must entertain each other in brotherly affection, we must be willing to abridge ourselves of our superfluities for the supply of others' necessities, we must uphold a familiar commerce together in all meekness, gentleness, patience, and liberality, we must delight in each other, make others' conditions our own, rejoice together, mourn together, labor and suffer together. . . ."

John Winthrop, on board the *Arbella*
en route to New England, 1630

CONTENTS

FOREWORD

Nothing is more mysterious or more obvious, more fragile or more durable, than what holds us Americans together. For by community we overcome the beast in us and become one with our neighbors; yet in community, too, we combine and organize our hates. A community may last for millennia, and yet may be shattered in decades. A community must be held together by ideas and words, and yet can be split by clenched fists. A community is, to paraphrase Pascal, "but a reed, the most feeble thing in nature." But by combining our best thoughts and better feelings we become a "thinking reed," and so rise above our age and above ourselves.

When the earliest promoters of America called this a "New Eden" they meant not only that America was a delightful place, but that it was where men could find new ways of living together. On the whole, their hopes have been fulfilled. Our civilization has brought men into new communities and has discovered new possibilities in old communities. In this, our twentieth century has been fantastically productive, far more than we have acknowledged or given ourselves credit for. The new-style American communities—in which men somehow feel their similarity, their kinship, their common interests, common problems, and common goals—are so pervasive that we hardly notice them. And they are so novel that people elsewhere have not even recognized them as communities.

In this volume I begin by exploring some of these new-style communities. Our new ways of thinking about and classifying ourselves, our myriad new products and services offered in unimagined quantities, our new ways of advertising and distributing, our new institutions for promoting philanthropy, the arts, and education, our American Standard of Living—almost everything most modern and most American has drawn us together in unprecedented ways.

In the second part of this volume I suggest how the very agencies which draw us together also stir Americans to fear, to distrust, and even to hate, one another. The new American communities are more numerous and more pervasive than those which in the past have held people together. But they are also thinner, more volatile, more transient. If we share more experiences with other Americans, the experiences which we share and the very sense of sharing are far less intense than ever before.

The old radicalisms were themselves rooted in a sense of sharing. But nowadays those who pass for "radicals" are in fact desperate *ego*litarians. They lack the sense of community and in them we witness the decline of radicalism.

As everything about our lives becomes more attenuated, as central heating and air conditioning assimilate winter and summer, as canning and deepfreezing homogenize the diets of the seasons, as television reduces the difference between being here and being there (so that sometimes we are more there when we are here than when we are there!), our whole world is flattened out. We then go anxiously in quest of that poignancy of sensation which our grandfathers felt in a warm fire on a winter's hearth or in the juicy bite of a summer peach. We self-consciously seek the old intensity of feeling when men were held together mainly or mostly by shared religious or political faiths or by shared fears of starvation, plague, or death.

"Newsworthiness"—a byproduct of our wealth and literacy—has become the test of what reaches us. Dramatic televisability has become the test of what we see and think about ourselves. Consequently our picture of our America becomes more and more distorted. We see the rifts and fissures, the bloody heads, the growling police dogs, the screaming mobs, while forgetting that there can be no divisions unless there is something to divide.

It is not at all surprising then that some of our fellow Americans go in desperate quest of communities, though communities can never be the product of desperation. And without intending it, they produce anti-communities, held together by common hatreds and disgusts and frustrations. They imagine that the simple quest for power—for student power, "black" power, or some other kind of power—can replace the larger community. Their confident desperation is itself an unwitting symptom of our most traditional American hope.

While we have lived and prospered on compromise, we are, at this late day, in danger of becoming utopians. Nowadays the American passion for self-reform, and the conviction that our society has not been able to solve *all* problems, paralyzes us into a national amnesia—a forgetfulness of how many problems we really have solved. In a paroxysm of self-abasement, our respectable leaders acquiesce in the efforts of a few to cure past evils by creating present evils. For example, leaders today stand unresistant before naïve and often vicious efforts to combat the evils of past white racism by an equally evil and even more passionate black racism.

Homeopathic medicine, a fad of the early nineteenth century, declared that a disorder could be cured by giving people a small dose of drugs producing effects similar to the disorder. This notion has long since been discredited in physiology. But every day we see the increasing popularity and respectability of a homeopathic social science. It is built on a similar perverse principle in treating the ills of society. How can we cure the ills of segregation? By a little more segregation, of course! By encouraging the very people who have suffered most from segregation to give themselves (and the whole society) a "small dose" of a new segregation in "black" society! But if America is to survive, and to continue to fulfill its mission for man, we must see these dangers and expunge this social quackery. As the Nazi experience should have taught us, certain evils (and racism is one of them) cannot be administered in small doses. When people begin to believe that racism is useful medicine, they begin to make their disease incurable.

These essays have been written in years when the disruptions of American community have reached a peacetime climax. While four-letter obscenities have lost their stigma, many well-meaning Americans treat patriotism and affirmation as indecent words. Although I have written in an enquiring mood, my keynote for this book is a single word oddly forgotten in our later-twentieth-century America: Yes.

* * * *

While this book explores some peculiarities of America today, its mood is not topical but historical. My "scale of years"—like the scale of miles you find on a map—reads "one inch equals a decade."

I am mainly concerned not with current events but with the currents of history, with the shaping of a civilization. These chapters have been written over the last few years, and I have not tried to "update" them or to give them a specious topicality. While their aim is to discover the meaning of some of today's trivia, confusions, and passions, the meaning I seek is not for tomorrow but for our generation and our children's. If my suggestions are helpful, they may somehow help us see our whole history and our problems and possibilities as a civilization. At the risk of seeming cryptic, I have preferred to let the reader himself discover, or test, the book's relevance to this morning's newspaper.

ONE

☆　　☆

I

THE RISE
 OF THE
AVERAGE MAN

Ours is a society of numbers. We are by all odds the most numbered, the most numerated, the most frequently and variously counted people in history. There was a time when only convicts (whom society was trying to punish by depriving of their identity) were identified by number. Nowadays it is by our identifying numbers that we all secure our identity. If we are young we must remember our Selective Service number. If we want our unemployment compensation or old-age payments or Medicare, we must recall our Social Security number. To pay for what we or our automobile consumes we must have our credit card number. Friends wanting to reach us promptly by mail must have our Zip Code number. Even our telephone numbers have become purely numerical.

But these are only symptoms. They signal a new numerical way of looking at man, a new way of looking at ourselves. To understand American civilization in the latter part of the twentieth century, we must know what we have made of statistics; and what statistics have made of us. We must understand how a nation that was compounded of old-style communities—communities of Puritans crossing the ocean sharing theology and hopes to build in New England a City upon a Hill, of wagon-companies moving westward through the continent-ocean sharing hopes for a better life somewhere, of settlers in quick-growing upstart cities (St. Louis, Omaha, Denver, Chicago, San Francisco, Kansas City) sharing their booster faith, of neighborhood communities of farmers who met weekly at the village post office to collect their scanty mail—how these became a twentieth-century America of new kinds of communities.

Ours, too, are communities of shared hopes, of a vividly shared present, and of shared expectations. But they differ from the older communities in many ways. They are fragmented, and they are everywhere. What holds members of these new communities together is not a shared religious or civic dogma, not a shared booster-enthusiasm, not even a shared economic interest, but something much vaguer and more attenuated. It is a shared consciousness, a shared awareness. People now think of themselves as members of groups and classes which were unimagined only a century ago. These groups give our society much of its special flavor in this century.

Among the most novel and most important are those which I call "Statistical Communities." The creatures of no ancient beliefs, of no consistent doctrine, they are a kind of byproduct of the religion of science stated in the divine language of numbers. They are the increasingly conscious product of the sciences and technology of a federal, democratic, literate society, which has come to measure its material well-being not by the Old World yardstick of wealth, but by the New World, blatantly public, Standard of Living.

They are creatures of a vast new democracy of consumers in an expanding nation.

HOW WE BECAME STATISTICALLY MINDED

The shape of American politics committed us, from our national beginnings, to a special interest in numbers. In one of the great compromises at the Philadelphia constitutional convention of 1787 the large and the small states agreed upon a two-branch federal legislature: one, a Senate where each state would be equally represented; another, a House of Representatives where the people would be represented according to their numbers. (Art. I, sec. 2, para. 3) "The actual Enumeration shall be made within three Years after the first Meeting of the Congress of the United States, and within every subsequent Term of ten Years, in such Manner as they shall by Law direct." The federal census was not the first such headcount, for within the previous two centuries there had been official counts in Virginia, in New France (later Quebec), and in Sweden, among others. But our periodic national census was probably the first in modern times to become institutionalized, and the American example influenced the world.

Elaboration of the federal census was a byproduct of the internal struggle which culminated in the Civil War. Before 1850 the United States census was a pretty amateurish institution and its product was rudimentary. The census of 1790 gave nothing but total population, divided into white (male and female) and colored (free and slave); white males were divided into those above and below sixteen years of age. Even before the second census, a movement headed by the American Philosophical Society (led by Vice-President Jefferson) urged the enlarging of its scope. Consequently, the Census of 1800 broke down the white population (male and female) into five age groups. Until 1850, census data were gathered according to judicial districts by federal marshals and their assistants who had had no experience in such matters. The unit of information was not the individual but the family.

In 1850, the official statistics of the United States began to enter the modern era. The epoch-making Seventh Census of that year was the product of a symbolic collaboration between James D. B. DeBow, a southern partisan, long interested in the diversification of the southern economy, who viewed statistics as a tool in the building of his section and of the nation, and Lemuel Shattuck of Massachusetts, a pioneer in improving laws requiring the registration of vital statistics, an enthusiast for the use of statistics in promoting education and public health. Now for the first time statistics were reported not for families but for individuals. Local census-takers merely filled out forms, which were forwarded to a central office in Washington for uniform tabulation and classification. The first six federal censuses had been confined, for all practical purposes, to a counting of the population. Now many new facts were gathered about the social and economic life of the nation: on the products of agriculture and industry, on schools and colleges, churches, libraries, newspapers and periodicals, pauperism, crime, and wages. The census had become a national inventory.

The sectional debate over slavery was a battle not only of lawyers, politicians, ministers, moralists, and novelists, but also of statisticians. Numbers seemed to offer self-evident answers to complicated social questions. From the raw material of the Census of 1850, Hinton R. Helper, a North Carolinian, made his *Impending Crisis of the South* (1857), which was probably the most influential anti-slavery work of non-fiction. The Republican party ordered one hundred thousand copies to support Lincoln in the campaign of 1860.

Other peculiarities of the American situation had reenforced the interest in statistics. The new communities here discovered a power to experiment with public health for which there was no precedent in the Old World. As early as 1721–22 the Boston smallpox epidemic and the trials of inoculation occasioned a pioneering statistical analysis. Promotional brochures had long boasted of the peculiar salubriousness of the American air, soil, and water. Jefferson's *Notes on Virginia* (1784) used statistics to refute European slanders against the animal and human products of America. The booster-enthusiasm which once nourished legends of an American Fountain of Youth, led latter-day city-promoters to use figures real or imaginary to prove that in their place people lived longer, and everything desirable was bigger and more numerous.

The words "Statistics" and "Statistical" entered the language in England about 1790, probably from the German. It was a symptom of expanding nationalism and of a widespread and growing faith in measurement and in all sorts of new sciences. In origin the words were somehow associated with the "State." In 1797, the *Encyclopaedia Britannica* (3d ed.) defined, *"Statistics,* a word lately introduced to express a view of any kingdom, county, or parish." Its meaning quickly broadened. "The idea I annex to the term," the far-sighted Sir John Sinclair wrote in 1798, "is an inquiry into the state of a country, for the purpose of ascertaining the quantum of happiness enjoyed by its inhabitants, and the means of its future improvement." The great European figure in the practical science of statistics, who extended its scope, and aroused the interest of non-specialists, was a Belgian mathematician and astronomer, Adolphe Quetelet (1796–1874). Having helped organize Holland's pioneer census of 1829, he later elaborated enticing new notions of "moral statistics" and "social physics," and proposed the encompassing concept of *l'homme moyen,* or the average man.

Americans, with plenty of reasons of their own to be interested in the quantities of everything, were not immune to these new scientific enthusiasms. The American Statistical Association, founded in Boston in 1839, set itself the task of collecting, interpreting, and diffusing statistics "as general and as extensive as possible and not confined to any particular part of the country." At the Association's seventy-fifth anniversary in 1914, Dr. S. N. D. North, the first head of a permanent census office (founded in 1902), divided all modern history "into two periods, the non-statistical and the statistical; one the period of superstition, the other the period of ascertained facts expressed in numerical terms. . . . The science of statistics is the chief instrumentality through which the progress of civilization is now measured, and by which its development hereafter will be largely controlled."

Meanwhile, one of the crucial inventions of the modern age, without which the vast proliferation of Statistical Communities would not have been possible, was made by an unsung American pioneer, Dr. Herman Hollerith. His system of punched holes on a non-conducting card which counted items by allowing an electric current to pass through the holes identically placed, was perfected in time for the federal Census of 1890. It was not only a great labor-saver, but finally made possible complex correlations. Now it was as easy to tabulate the number of married carpenters forty to forty-five years of age as to tabulate the total number of persons forty to forty-five years of age. Hollerith's simple invention was the grandparent of the modern computer industry; his enterprise became part of the International Business Machines Corporation which, with other similar firms, has made the hum of the computer heard throughout the land.

Numerous techniques for visualizing statistics, dramatizing them for the wider public, were developed at the same time. Dr. Henry Gannett, a geographer, used novel and ingenious means for symbolizing census results in his Statistical Atlases for the Censuses of 1890 and 1900. Further advances were made by cartographers for newsmagazines in this century. A growing popular demand for current statistics on all sorts of subjects, from railroads to books, produced many new statistical almanacs. One of the most useful and most influential of these, since its first appearance in 1878, was the annual *Statistical Abstract of the United States*. It has become the standard national inventory— social, political, economic, and cultural—and is a statistical treasurehouse for everybody, as it leaves no part of our national life untouched.

THE RISE OF STATISTICAL COMMUNITIES

We could not have developed our Statistical Communities —our new ways of thinking about ourselves—if we had not been flooded in the last century with facts, and especially with figures about ourselves. For Statistical Communities have come into being from personal discovery followed by public awareness that large numbers of people share certain specific characteristics. The rise of statistics during the nineteenth century of course produced a vast theoretical literature, to which Americans contributed. Our concern here, however, is not with the heated controversies that raged in the learned societies and among professors, but rather with the new light in which laymen now saw themselves.

How did Statistical Communities begin to be formed?

How did they develop? At least five new forces in American life since the Civil War have helped create and shape Statistical Communities.

1. *The rise of ready-made clothing and the growth of the science of sizes.* While at the opening of the nineteenth century, perhaps nine Americans out of ten wore home-made clothing and only one wore tailor-made or factory-made clothing, at the end of the century the proportions were quite reversed. By then perhaps nine out of ten wore factory-made clothing, bought by mail order or in a store. Many facts help explain why this Clothing Revolution had not occurred before. One reason why, until the mid-nineteenth century, so little clothing was manufactured in quantity was the backwardness of "anthropometry," or the science of human measurements. It was generally assumed that every man's body was quite different from every other's and, therefore, that to try to manufacture large quantities of clothing which would actually fit their different wearers was futile. If one wanted a fit, one had to make his own clothing or secure a tailor. As late as 1850, nearly all manufactured shoes were "straights," made so that they would fit equally well (or badly) either the right or the left foot.

But the Civil War, with its great demand for military uniforms, produced a large fund of new information on the common dimensions of the human body. This disclosed the valuable fact that certain sets of measurements tended to recur with predictable regularity. At the end of the war, these measurements guided manufacturers who were supplying civilian garments: to the hundreds of thousands of demobilized soldiers; to the flood of new immigrants; to the prospering inhabitants of the mushrooming cities like Chicago, Omaha, and Denver; and to the rising workmen who themselves were securing higher wages in thousands of new factories. In 1880 appeared Daniel Edward Ryan's epoch-making book, *Human Proportions in Growth: Being the Complete Measurement of the Human Body for Every Age and Size during the Years of Juvenile Growth,* the first scientific guide for standardizing measurements in men's, boys' and juveniles' ready-made clothing. Others followed. Before long a man could walk into a clothing store, indicate that he was a "42" and put on a jacket that (with little or no alteration) would satisfy a fastidious eye. People thus began to think of themselves as belonging to certain "sizes"—in shoes, shirts, suits, trousers, and hats. They had joined new Statistical Communities.

2. *The rise of the cash register, of income tax, and of income-consciousness.* In the same years when men were beginning to take a precise, statistical view of their bodies, they were beginning to take a similar new view of their incomes. Until well after the Civil War, only the rare merchant had an accurate record of his sales. Negligence, semi-literacy, and laziness made the record incomplete; few clerks were so scrupulous as actually to write everything down in the daybook. Where transactions were small and numerous, and where the sales clerk or bartender made change out of his own pocket or from an open cash box, clerks were tempted to pilfering. The merchant seldom knew precisely where he stood.

The device that did more than any other to change all this was the "cash register" (an American expression which entered the language about 1879). James Ritty, the principal inventor of the cash register, ran a café-saloon in Dayton, Ohio, where he made alarmingly small profits from what seemed to be a thriving business. Suspecting that his profits were going into the pockets of his bartenders, he devised a rudimentary cash register (called "Ritty's Incorruptible Cashier"), first patented in 1879. It was gradually improved to include an indicator publicly displaying the amount of each transaction, a paper roll recording the day's sales, and a cash drawer opened only by depressing a key, which also rang a bell. Within only a few decades, the official history of the National Cash Register Company boasts, this bell, "like the historic Revolutionary shot fired at Lexington . . . would be heard round the world." This was hardly an exaggeration, for Ritty's invention came into the hands of John Henry Patterson, whose genius for organization and for the higher strategy of salesmanship (he pioneered a system of guaranteed territories and of sales-quotas) made the National Cash Register Company a model of American enterprise. Before Patterson's death in 1922, his "Gospel of Making Proper Financial Records" had made millions of converts and the cheery ring of the cash register was heard even in village stores.

Like other innovations in twentieth-century America, the cash register helped make shopping a public and communal activity. It also helped make a revolution in accounting among small merchants and in service occupations, and promoted efficiency in department stores, chain stores, and supermarkets by the new data of multi-totals, by the classification of transactions according to size, sales person, and department. For the first time, reliable statistics about an individual business enabled the merchant to figure precisely his annual profit or loss.

The kind of information which the cash register provided the individual merchant was increasingly required of more and more Americans with the rise of the income tax. "Until the income tax was established," Claude C. Hopkins, the advertising pioneer, recalled in 1927, "I kept no record of my earnings. Their volume meant nothing to me." Many less prosperous and less money-minded Americans were equally vague about their earnings. They had only the crudest notion of what "income group" they belonged to. But after the adoption of the Income Tax Amendment (the 16th) to the Constitution in 1913, things were different. By the mid-1960's over a third of the population (and over one half those of voting age) were filing income-tax returns. Millions were now forced to think of themselves as members of an income-class. They shared a similar burden of taxation with others in their $5,000-a-year or $10,000-a-year, or whatever-a-year bracket. As the social sciences grew, and were popularized and vulgarized, increasing numbers of Americans were more and more frequently reminded of additional characteristics that they shared with others in these Statistical Communities.

3. *Immigration, and the counting and classifying of newcomers.* The word "immigrant," an Americanism introduced around 1789, was described by an early English traveler as "perhaps the only new word, of which the circumstances of the United States has in any degree demanded the addition to the English language." But official statistics on immigration were not kept before 1820. Only gradually, during the nineteenth century, did Americans become statistically conscious of the immigrant. Shattuck boasted that his pioneer Boston census of 1845 had first distinguished "the native from the foreign population." In 1850 the federal census began to classify the white population into "native" and "foreign born." As the flood of immigrants widened and deepened, and as these immigrants clustered in large enclaves, many of the most respectable, and even of the reform-minded "native" Americans became alarmed. The Immigration Restriction League, founded in Boston in 1894 under Harvard Brahmin leadership, soon received support from many leading figures in New England literature and public life—including Henry Cabot Lodge, John Fiske, Albert Bushnell Hart, Thomas Bailey Aldrich, Barrett Wendell, and Abbott Lawrence Lowell. Comfortable New Eng-

landers, bewildered by "labor troubles" and the increasing complexity of American Life, drew on recently gathered statistics (the federal census of 1880 listed 15,000,000 immigrants; the Massachusetts census of 1885 classified over 63 per cent of Bostonians as foreign by birth or parentage) to explain their problems. There were numerous studies, like Henry Cabot Lodge's "Distribution of Ability in the United States," which was a statistical analysis of *Appleton's Cyclopaedia of American Biography* proving that since the adoption of the Constitution, from Great Britain alone had come "three-fourths of the ability furnished from outside sources."

The immigration issue, like the slavery issue before it, was translated into a statistical question; and was finally to be "resolved" in a system of statistical quotas. Those on all sides of the question gathered figures in a host of ill-defined categories: "literacy," "temperance," "pauperism," "insanity," "feeble-mindedness," "anarchism," "communism" —as well as on prostitution, polygamy, and criminal convictions. Private surveys and government reports abounded. One of the most extensive was the Report of the Immigration Commission of 1907 (42 vols., 1911) which was a monument to the prejudices of the day, but which also collected much valuable information in statistical form. Statistical surveys were also directed to stemming the movement from the country to the city, and to numerous other problems. Out of these and other studies came the newly restrictive immigration policy of the United States in the twentieth century. And there also came a new awareness among Americans generally of their membership in statistical groups defined by national origin, religion, and mother-tongue, which were now cast into Statistical Communities.

4. *The rise of intelligence-tests, personality-tests, and personnel-mindedness.* The interest in eugenics and genetics

which early in the nineteenth century had helped found a new science of statistics, later in the century stirred an interest in tests which were supposed to measure objectively differences in human intelligence and performance. Two Frenchmen, Alfred Binet and Theodore Simon, developed new ways of scoring tests and devised a scale of intelligence in 1905 for classifying the children in Paris schools into normal and subnormal. Their scale was translated into English and introduced into the United States in 1908. Then, in 1912, William Stern, a German psychologist who later immigrated to this country, proposed an Intelligence Quotient ("mental age" divided by chronological age), soon popularly known as I.Q. This notion was adopted by the American psychologist Lewis M. Terman, who with collaborators at Stanford University in 1918 produced a revision of the Binet-Simon tests, which in one form or another still dominates the field in the United States. This was only a beginning.

Then came tests (by Arnold Gesell and others) for infants and young children. The problems of recruitment in World War I provided the occasion for tests which could be administered to large numbers at once. During that war, intelligence tests were administered to over a million and a half recruits. Tests proliferated—for "aptitude," "will-temperament," "social intelligence," "aggressiveness," "cooperation," and scores of other traits. Statistical inventories of qualities of the individual paralleled the statistical inventories of the nation and its resources. "Personality," once replete with metaphysical overtones, took on a new primary meaning to describe the whole of a person's outwardly classifiable traits. It became the subject matter of new sciences, the raw material of new tests, and the data of new statistics. Inevitably, then, the new "personnel administration" (by about 1912 at least a dozen large American corporations had grouped activities under such a heading) was both a symptom and a cause of the tendency to treat employees as data testable and classifiable into statistical categories.

Tests became a mania and a pastime. Magazines like *Time* and *Newsweek* offered readers periodic tests of "knowledge of current affairs." By 1965, the Columbia Broadcasting Corporation televised a series of Citizenship Tests, using newspapers to provide scoring sheets, so that viewers could discover, at the end of the program, to which percentile of the population they belonged. National Merit scholarships and others open to nation-wide competition gave a new prominence to test scores and percentile ratings, reenforced by intensified competition for admission to the better colleges, also increasingly determined by College Entrance Examinations and other scores and percentiles. By the late 1960's more and more Americans (and especially the youth) were aware of their membership in Statistical Communities, signaled by intelligence, personality, or test-performance. People joked about their I.Q. and it entered into popular song.

5. *The rise of market research and of opinion polling.* Statistical Communities began to be formed even of people who shared passing whims, casual prejudices, or ill-informed attitudes, who lacked a certain kind of knowledge, who had "no opinion" on a subject, or who merely liked or disliked some celebrity. Scientific opinion polling arose as a byproduct of advertising. Market surveys were devised about 1912 by Roy O. Eastman to find out who was reading the magazines in which his breakfast food was advertised. By 1919 a survey department had appeared in an advertising agency, and then came the independent survey organizations. Market research techniques were applied to public issues in 1935. *Fortune* was the first to publish widely the results of such surveys (under Elmo Roper and others); and

soon George Gallup was syndicating his features, regularly offering newspaper readers statistics on what proportion of the population favored or opposed this or that attitude, or had "no opinion." Political polls, further elaborated by Samuel Lubell, Louis Harris, and others, were taken so frequently and in such a variety of ways, that the voter no longer needed to await the official balloting to see with whom he shared his opinions. If a man intended to vote Republican, he could learn from the newspapers that this put him in the Statistical Community of 44 per cent of the farmers of a certain state, and of 55 per cent of the suburbanites of a certain city, and with this or that percentage of professional persons, white collar employees, or manual workers, and among the majority or minority of Protestants, Catholics, or Jews.

New Statistical Communities were forming and dissolving every day. A man could discover from the newspaper, radio, or television that merely to possess no opinion, on a topic of which he had never heard, would place him in a certain sharply defined Statistical Community.

Countless other factors have multiplied Statistical Communities. Insurance, of course, depends for its very existence on reliable statistics; and the great insurance companies like the Metropolitan Life Insurance Company of New York, while advancing actuarial science, have accumulated statistical information and spent large sums of money to remind citizens of how their most intimate daily habits—of smoking, of drinking, of exercise, and of sexual relations—might make them members of Statistical Communities. But not until after the Civil War was it common for Americans to carry life insurance. In 1860 only some 60,000 persons held life insurance policies; by 1910, ordinary life policies numbered nearly seven million, in addition to so-called "industrial" life policies (in small amounts, mainly to cover burial expenses) of which there were over twenty-three million. People buying life insurance were joining Statistical Communities, in which the cost of membership plainly depended on characteristics of the other members. Perhaps the most pervasive and increasingly powerful creator of new Statistical Communities was government—local, state, and federal. Social security, unemployment insurance, Medicare, and a host of other activities have increased occasions when the citizen is counted and classified, when he is reminded of sharing qualities and concerns with numbers of unseen fellow-Americans.

FROM FACTS TO NORMS:
THE MIRROR OF STATISTICS

More significant for American life than what we have made of statistics, is what they have made of us. Statistics began as a social inventory; in the century since the Civil War they have become for each of us a personal mirror. When Hinton R. Helper's *Impending Crisis of the South* (1857) pointed out that in the Free States there were 14,911 libraries containing 3,888,234 volumes, but in the Slave States there were only 695 libraries with 649,577 volumes, it was to contrast the two societies. Even when, eighty years later, President Franklin D. Roosevelt spoke of the "one-third of a nation" that was "ill-housed, ill-clad, and ill-nourished," he was still speaking the language of social inventory.

But statistics have tended to make facts into norms. A "norm," the dictionary reminds us, is a "standard, model, or pattern." Nowadays when a California suburbanite calls himself a member of a "two-car family" he is using statistics as a mirror; he is putting himself in a Statistical Community, tactfully implying that he shares other characteristics with those other substantial Americans. When a parent (drawing on his Gesell) explains the fidgitiness of his three-year-old child by saying that most children of that age have a short attention-span, he is plainly making the figures into a model.

More and more Americans, in more and more departments of their lives, look to statistics not merely for facts but for norms. They look at (and for) themselves in the social mirror. By making the fact the norm, we all make it somehow the law, the measure, and the external deposit of our moral life. We make the "is" the substance and not merely the shadow of the "ought." A genius for vagueness, a talent for mingling the future with the present, has characterized much of American life—from the promotional tracts of the colonial period through the booster press of the upstart cities of the early nineteenth century into the advertising tall talk of the twentieth century. We Americans have habitually confused "is" with "ought," fact with desire, self with society.

It is no wonder that statistics, which first secured prestige here by a supposedly impartial utterance of stark fact, have enlarged their dominion over the American consciousness by becoming the most powerful statements of the "ought"—displacers of moral imperatives, personal ideals, and unfulfilled objectives. They are the symbol of the world as it is; they have become the model for the world as it might be, of the "ought" imprisoned in the "is," of the ideal imprisoned in the image. Is it any wonder that there should be a deepening doubt of the desirability of Walt Whitman's "Divine Average"—the equalitarian ideal—when we see it as the creature no longer of God but of the statisticians?

II

WELCOME

TO THE

 CONSUMPTION

COMMUNITY

People tell us we are a *rich* nation. And that what distinguishes us is our *high* standard of living. But an Old World vocabulary conceals what is most radically distinctive about our material well-being. It is not that we are well off; there have been rich nations before us. It is not that we have a *high* standard of living. What is different is our very notion of a standard of living, and our New World way of thinking about and consuming material goods.

The movement from the Old World to the New was a movement from an ancient and traditional view of wealth to the new view that goes by the name of standard of living. "Wealth," which was at the center of English mercantilist economic thinking before the American Revolution, was a static notion. The wealth of the world, which was measured primarily in gold and silver, was supposed to be a fixed quantity. It was a pie that could be sliced one way or another. But the size of the pie could not be substantially increased. A bigger slice for Great Britain meant a smaller slice for France or Spain or somebody else, and one nation's gain was another's loss.

The New World changed that way of thinking. People who came to live here came to better their lot in the world, to improve their "way of life." They sought opportunities to rise, to get some land, to think and speak freely, to move, to worship, to secure more education, to grow. By contrast with the European view, America bred a vaguer and much more expansive view of the material world.

The American Revolution itself was among other things a struggle between two different concepts of wealth. Britain stood for the older, more rigid view of wealth. Autarky—economic self-sufficiency—was the ideal of national power. But this way of thinking was uncongenial to the New World. The indefinite expanse of a half-known and temperate continent opened unimagined possibilities for nearly everybody. "Strangers are welcome," Franklin explained in his *Information to Those Who Would Remove to America* (1782), "because there is room enough for them all, and therefore the old inhabitants are not jealous of them."

Americans were not merely struggling for their slice of the pie, every day they were actually making the pie bigger. The indefinite expansibility of material wealth was an American axiom, never abandoned. The Old World's notions about what was material well-being, what was worth fighting about, were becoming obsolete.

In the Old World poverty was one of the inescapable facts of life. Those who wished to justify God's design even said that poverty was not without its social benefits, since it made charity possible. The American view was different. The advantages of poverty, Andrew Carnegie explained in 1891, were mainly to provide the conditions for young men to rise in the world and become wealthy. The ideal self-made man was the man who rose, not at the expense of others, but while building new communities where others would flourish. The slogans of "The New Freedom," "The New Deal," "The New Frontier," and "The Great Society" have carried these hopes forward into the twentieth century.

With this novel, vague, and expansive view of material well-being came a new way of talking about the wealth of the society. This new view was *communitarian*. Its focus was not on riches but on the way of life, not on the individual but on the community. Or, rather, on many novel kinds of communities. One of these, which came to dominate the twentieth century, was the byproduct of innovation in manufacturing and distributing things. To it I give the name "Consumption Community." A Consumption Community is held together by much thinner, more temporary ties than those that bound earlier Americans. It does not replace earlier kinds of communities. But it draws together in novel ways people who would not otherwise have been drawn together—people who do not share ideology, who are not voyaging together on the prairie or building new towns. It is a hallmark of American life today.

WHAT MADE CONSUMPTION COMMUNITIES

A Consumption Community consists of people who have a feeling of shared well-being, shared risks, common interests, and common concerns that come from consuming the same kinds of objects. It can be the community of Scotch drinkers who rally to the J & B brand, of three-button-suit wearers, of Chevrolet sports-car drivers, of super-king-sized cigarette smokers, or of Doublemint gum chewers. As the advertisers of nationally branded and nationally advertised products are constantly telling us, by buying their products we are joining a special group—the Dodge Rebellion, the Pepsi Generation, those who throw in their lot with Avis because it is only No. 2. And each of us eagerly joins many such groups. Yet we are slow to admit that buying these products and services actually puts us into novel—extremely attenuated, yet characteristically American—communities.

We remain imprisoned in an old-fashioned vocabulary. We still talk as if we were back in the world of the gunsmith who made his gun to suit a particular customer, in the days when nearly everybody wore home-made clothing and the few who wore store-boughten suits patronized a custom tailor. The world of the consumer and the experience of the consumer have not yet been given the dignity of "community." We readily speak of religious communities and political communities, but we have not yet learned to think of the consumer as belonging to communities or to speak of Consumption Communities.

Consumption Communities could not come into being until there were large numbers of objects being made that were, from the consumer's point of view, indistinguishable from one another. So long as a man purchased his gun from his own gunsmith, who had made the object for him alone, his use and enjoyment of his gun could not tie him to very many other people. Each gun—like other custom-made objects, such as suits or shoes—was designed partly by the buyer, and then made by the craftsman to the buyer's specifications. But when Whitney or Colt or a large manufacturing concern in Springfield began making guns, and making them in standard models by the thousands, every buyer of a Whitney or a Colt or a Springfield was risking his money (and sometimes, too, his life) with many others. American industry prospered on more and more ways of making precisely similar objects.

The needs of a large army in the Civil War produced masses of similar items, and after the war the new way of making things created the early Consumption Communities.

Before the Civil War it was widely assumed that well-fitting clothes could not be manufactured in large quantities since everybody was supposed to be a different size. But makers of uniforms found that, among large numbers of men, certain sizes recurred in a regular way; this laid the foundation for a science of "anthropometry." By the time of the publication in 1880 of Daniel Edward Ryan's *Human Proportions in Growth,* the factory-made clothing industry was on its way. For the first time in modern history it became possible for thousands of men of all social classes to wear clothing of the same design, cut, and manufacture, coming from a central factory. Before the end of the nineteenth century all but a small proportion of American men were wearing store-boughten clothing.

The making of large numbers of similar objects gradually extended to all items of consumption. Cigarettes, which until the later nineteenth century had been mostly hand-made, were now rolling off speedy new machines that, by the 1930's, were producing about 150 billion per year. Foods, soft drinks, and gadgets of all kinds were soon available in identical forms and in quantities that by the early twentieth century had dominated the lives of most Americans. And the supreme achievement of precise mass production was, of course, the automobile, which soon became the omnipresent symbol of American Consumption Communities. By the third decade of the century, the house that a man lived in, together with antiques and certain art works (and the land that he lived on), were almost the only objects that had not become fungible—readily replaced in the market by others that were indistinguishable.

This capacity to produce millions of similar objects was necessary to the creation of Consumption Communities. But it was not enough. Community requires a *consciousness* of community. And at the same time, in the century after the Civil War, there grew in America new institutions that made men and women aware of their membership in Consumption Communities. Two large developments brought the new consciousness into being.

First came the retailing revolution. Its two principal novel agents were the department store and the mail-order house. Before the middle of the nineteenth century, city dwellers bought their goods from numerous specialized shops, each offering a relatively small stock of one kind of commodity—drygoods, hardware, groceries, crockery, or tableware. Then, in 1846, A. T. Stewart in New York City pioneered with his Marble Dry-Goods Palace at Broadway and Chambers Street. He gave a hint of the vastness and grandeur of the new retailing enterprises with his new multistory building in 1862, which became famous as Stewart's Cast Iron Palace. Others, too—R. H. Macy in New York, John Wanamaker in Philadelphia and New York, Marshall Field and Carson Pirie Scott in Chicago, and many more—combined their pioneering in large-scale retailing with pioneering in architecture.

To the entering customer they opened new perspectives: long vistas of appealing merchandise. These attracted numerous clusters of buyers, shoppers, and just lookers. And these were displayed not in the motley disorder of a country fair, but as the common offering of a single great enterprise. A buyer at Stewart's or Macy's or Wanamaker's was not simply confiding in the integrity of a particular shopkeeper. He was joining a large community of consumers, all of whom put their confidence (and their cash) in the same large firm. When the one-price system, popularized by R. H. Macy, took the place of the ancient custom of haggling, buyers more than ever were sharing their confidence in the merchant.

What the department store was to the city dweller, the

mail-order house was to the farmer. Montgomery Ward, which had begun only in 1872, issued a catalogue for 1884 that numbered 240 pages and listed over 10,000 items. Sears, Roebuck & Co., which had started as a one-man mail-order watch business in 1886, was grossing over $50 million by 1907, selling every shape and size of merchandise. In that year catalogue circulation already exceeded three million. The Ward and Sears catalogues, full of vivid illustrations (soon printed in color, in the development of which the mail-order houses were pioneers), opened the outside world to many lonely farm families. Thousands wrote in for personal advice. Buyers from the catalogue were putting their confidence in a firm located in a far-off city. It was no accident that the catalogue came to be called "the farmer's Bible." Men remote from one another found in their Sears catalogue a common iconography. They were tied together somehow by their common involvement in the large community of Sears customers.

At the same time there grew nationwide chains of poor man's department stores, 5-and-10-cent stores selling thousands of standardized small items. The customers of F. W. Woolworth shared the belief that these items could nowhere be bought more cheaply, and that they were good value for the money. This expanding confidence of the growing community of 5-and-10 customers within a few decades built what was at that time the highest building in the United States.

People who shopped at Stewart's, Macy's, Wanamaker's, or Marshall Field's, or who mailed in their orders to Ward or Sears, could see and feel that they had entered a new community of consumers. But another new force was reaching out into the city and the country, tying other groups of consumers together. It used the pages of newspapers and magazines, and the painted sides of barns, signs along the road, trolley cars and buses and commuter trains, and ultimately smoke writing in the sky, and words and music and images on the airwaves of radio and television. Before the middle of the twentieth century empty spaces everywhere were being filled with words and pictures, and the channels were crammed with words and music and pictures—designed to enlist new consumers into new Consumption Communities, and to keep old consumers loyal to the Consumption Communities they had joined. This new force was, of course, advertising.

ADVERTISING DISPLACES SALESMANSHIP

There are crucial differences between selling to a single buyer and creating a community of buyers. Different arguments become effective and different satisfactions are received by everyone concerned. The primary argument of the salesman is personal and private: this hat is perfect for *you* (singular). The primary argument of the advertisement is public and general: this hat is perfect for *you* (plural). The salesman is effective when he persuades the customer that the item is peculiarly suited to his unique needs. The advertisement is effective when it persuades groups of buyers that the item is well suited to the needs of all persons in the group. The salesman's focus is on the individual; he succeeds when he manages, cajoles, flatters, and overwhelms the ego. The advertisement's focus is on some group; it succeeds when it discovers, defines, and persuades persons who can be brought into that community of consumers.

A buyer who gives in to a salesman has satisfied his ego. But a consumer who is persuaded by an advertisement is also yielding to his desire or willingness to be counted in a group—a community of consumers. An advertisement is, in fact, a form of insurance to the consumer that by buying this commodity, by smoking this brand of cigarette, or by driving this make of car he will not find himself alone. The larger the advertising campaign, the more widespread and the more effective, the more the campaign itself offers a kind of communitarian seal of approval. Surely a million customers can't be wrong! An advertisement, then, is a kind of announcement that, in the well-informed judgment of experts, some kind of Consumption Community probably exists. Won't you join?

Advertising—the conscious effort to create Consumption Communities—did not become an important element in the economy and in securing customers until about a century ago. Patent medicines were the first to advertise on a national scale. But the use of display type and illustrations in daily newspaper advertising came in only slowly. As late as 1847, James Gordon Bennett, the otherwise enterprising editor of the New York *Herald,* banned all ornamental cuts. He believed in a typographic democracy, thinking it "unfair" to allow any advertiser an advantage over others by using display type. Bennett insisted that an advertiser should gain his advantage only from what he said, not from how it was printed. But by the later nineteenth century, newspaper and magazine pages were responding freely to the needs of advertisers. In 1879, Wanamaker placed what is said to be the first full-page American daily newspaper advertisement for a retail store. In the early twentieth century, display type, illustrations, and the full-page advertisement became commonplace.

The volume of national expenditure on advertising has increased spectacularly and regularly, interrupted only by the deeper depressions. In 1867 the total national figure was only some $50 million; by 1900 it had increased tenfold to half a billion dollars; by 1950 it had reached five and a half billion; by 1966 it was over sixteen billion. Since the 1930's, national advertising has increased more rapidly than local advertising. By 1966 the annual expenditure on local advertising was only about half that on national advertising. Brand names first flourished about the time of the Civil War with patent medicines, soaps, and cleaning powders. By the time of World War I, people were asking for national brands in chewing gum, watches, hats, breakfast food, razor blades, and pianos. Advertising was becoming a technique, a science, and a profession. In 1869 appeared Rowell's *American Newspaper Directory,* the first serious attempt to list all newspapers in the United States with accurate and impartial estimates of their circulation. Ayer's *American Newspaper Annual* followed in 1880.

The advertising agency then appeared, to guide manufacturers to the most effective use of the media. N. W. Ayer & Son of Philadelphia—which had started with a list of eleven religious newspapers before 1877—was a pioneer, but many others followed. Ayer's accounts included Hires root beer, Montgomery Ward, Procter & Gamble soaps, and Burpee seeds. By 1900 the advertising of foodstuffs held first place in the firm's volume. What was perhaps the biggest single advertising push until then was Ayer's campaign, beginning in January, 1899, for the new National Biscuit Co. This was one of the first campaigns to feature a staple food, nationally branded, boxed in individual packages, and ready for consumption. The campaign required the perfecting of an airtight package, and above all the popularizing of a distinctive trademark and brand name. Ayer reached consumers through newspapers, magazines, streetcar ads, posters, and painted signs. Overnight people all over the country were demanding the "Uneeda Biscuit."

Too much of the discussion of advertising has treated it as simply another form of salesmanship. Estimates of its social value have centered around its cost as a selling device, its relation to planned obsolescence and to other aspects of production. We must begin to realize that Consumption Communities actually offer many of the satisfactions that were once associated only with other kinds of groups.

A DEMOCRACY OF CASH

In its primary sense, a "community" was a group of people living together, under all the same conditions of life. In origin it appears to have come from the Latin *com* (together) plus the Latin *munus* (service, office, function, or duty)—hence meaning persons who paid taxes together or worked together. By extension it came to mean persons held together by some one common interest or concern, generally political or religious. In its primary sense, as in the New England community, or the New York community, or the plantation community, it meant persons who lived in geographic proximity. But it has also come to mean any group (the business community, the Catholic community, the Negro community, the Jewish community, the teen-age community, the suburban community) aware of its common character, and somehow held together, even though its members do not necessarily live close to one another.

Groups which we commonly call "communities" show the following characteristics: (a) people are aware that the membership gives them some common interests or concerns, (b) people are more or less free to enter or leave the community (if only by emigration), (c) people show more or less loyalty to some common object.

The peculiar importance of Consumption Communities in recent America helps us understand, too, how it has been possible here to assimilate—to "Americanize"—the many millions who have come within the last century and a half. Consumption Communities helped hold together as Americans people who in the older world would have been bound mainly by distinctions of class, ideology, or ancestry.

Here are some of the peculiarities of Consumption Communities—by contrast with other kinds of communities.

1. *Consumption Community is quick.* It takes generations to become an Englishman, one can never become a Frenchman. But, through joining Consumption Communities, immigrants have found it easy to become Americans. In his *Rise of David Levinsky* (1917), Abraham Cahan recounts how Jewish immigrants who arrived in New York City in the 1880's, feeling uneasily foreign, became quickly Americanized by buying ready-made clothes, by getting an American haircut, and by purchasing all kinds of small commodities, which were the signs of being a genuine American. The shrewd F. W. Woolworth, expanding his chain of 5-and-10-cent stores in the 1890's, consciously directed them toward this market of the newly arrived who wanted to buy like Americans.

2. *Consumption Community is non-ideological.* No profession of faith, no credo or orthodoxy, no ritual is required to join a Consumption Community. With only a few exceptions (now mostly having to do with housing), people of all races, beliefs, and religious and political creeds can join. And therefore:

3. *Consumption Community is democratic.* This is the great American democracy of cash, which so exasperates the aristocrats of all older worlds. Consumption Communities generally welcome people of all races, ancestries, occupations, and income levels, provided they have the price of admission. The boss and the worker both own a Westinghouse washer and both drive an Impala.

The Consumption Community is even more democratic than many a "democratic" political community. English law reformers used to say, "British justice, like the Ritz Hotel, is open to Rich and Poor alike." To secure a room in the Ritz, or in other de luxe London accommodations, though, you needed not only to have enough money but also to be a "gentleman" and to be a member of the right race. The struggle for "civil rights" in the United States has been in large part a struggle for the right to consume—a struggle to enlarge and complete the democracy of consumption. The purpose of the public-accommodation provisions of the Civil Rights Acts is to ensure that the Ritz Hotel and all other hotels, motels, and restaurants are open to whoever has the money.

People who want to protest against this peculiarly indiscriminate American democracy can do so only by under-consumption. It is possible, although increasingly inconvenient, to stay out of even the largest Consumption Communities. Latter-day Boston Brahmins must strain for exclusiveness by refusing to own an automobile or a television set. I have one such acquaintance who has the hardiness not to have a telephone—on the pretext that he is waiting for it to be perfected! The democracy of cash, even with all its present limitations in America, is probably one of the most real and present and unadulterated democracies in history.

4. *Consumption Communities tend to become the model of all other communities.* All experience tends to be treated more and more like the experience of consuming. It becomes the right of all citizens not merely to consume whatever they can afford to buy, but to consume it in the presence of (and in community with) all others who can afford to buy it. And of course we use advertising to create and strengthen old-style communities—communities of believers, religious and political.

FROM WEALTH TO STANDARD OF LIVING

The growth of Consumption Communities has signaled a transformation of the attitude to all material goods. By contrast with the rigid, Old World notion of wealth, the New World idea of standard of living has had certain obvious characteristics. I will mention only two.

Standard of living is public. But it is possible to be "wealthy" in secret. A man can hide his treasure in a vault, in his garden, in a mattress. "If rich, it is easy enough to conceal your wealth," an Englishman wrote in 1820, "for it is less difficult to hide a thousand guineas than a hole in your coat." It is not possible to have a high standard of living in secret.

The word "standard" (which comes into English from the Old French *estandard,* "banner") means a symbol that is displayed for all to see. Its very function is to be seen, to *inform* as much as to *affirm.* A standard of living, then, is a publicly seen and known measure of how people do live, and of how they should live. The first use of the phrase in its current and special American sense is obscure. But probably not until the twentieth century did the phrase come into widespread use with its present meaning.

The willingness of Americans to display their material well-being is rooted deep in our history. The fact that our homes front upon the street (and not inward to a court as did the middle-class homes of French and Spanish colonists), and that the symbols of urban residential comfort here are not the wall or the fence but the broad, open front lawn and the front porch—these are clues from small-town America of the last century. In mid-twentieth century, the Chrysler, Cadillac, or Continental conspicuously parked in front of the house offers new opportunities to show the well-being of the residents.

But the Americans' willingness to display their prosperity on the façades of their homes, through picture windows, on their lawns, and in the parking places in front of their houses, is by no means universal. Americans who travel the continent of Europe are sometimes shocked at the shabby exterior of the dwellings of well-to-do families of the middle class. The ancient institution of the tax farmer, who could estimate his exactions by the wealth displayed, put a premium on the ability to seem impecunious. An apocryphal story of the origin of the French state tobacco monopoly is a parable of the peculiarly Old World fear of displaying wealth. The story goes that to the Emperor Napoleon I, during one of his levees in Paris, there was presented a lady bedecked in diamonds and rubies. "How did you come by all this wealth?" the Emperor asked. "I am very lucky," she replied; "my husband is in the tobacco business." "How interesting," Napoleon retorted. "He isn't any more!"

But the United States was born in the principle of "No taxation without representation." The tax farmer has not been an American institution. We have been relatively free from social revolutions and from arbitrary confiscation. Americans have therefore had less reason to fear the consequences of public display of their wealth.

Because a high standard of living is a public fact, it becomes a public benefit. You can become *rich* without my becoming richer. But it is hard for you to have a high *standard of living* without incidentally raising mine. The rich classes of India, protected by their eight-foot stone walls, can enjoy luxury. They do not really have a high standard of living in the American sense so long as the squalor outside their walls threatens them with crime and disease. If, in addition to your material goods, your standard of living includes your freedom from threat of crime or disease, your education, the education of your children, the air you breathe, the water you drink, the roads you drive on, the public transportation system you use, your peace of mind— then does it not inevitably include *my* opportunities and the opportunities of *my* children for education (in the institutions you support), the air *I* breathe, the water *I* drink, the roads *I* drive on, the public transportation *I* use, and *my* freedom from threat of crime or disease?

Standard of living is pervasive, reciprocal, and communal. This plainly follows. Wealth is by definition what a man *possesses*. Property is what is "proper" to a person, peculiar or special to him. How obvious, then, that the wealth of some should explain the poverty of others. "The pleasures of the rich," wrote the Englishman Thomas Fuller, "are bought with the tears of the poor."

But standard of living is what a man *shares*. One man's standard of living cannot be sharply separated from that of others. Each person is part of everyone else's standard of living. You are my environment. And my environment is my standard of living. In a society that lives by a standard of living, no man is an island, for every man is part of every other man's standard of living. In a wealth society your gain is my loss; in a standard-of-living society your gain is my gain. If you live healthily I am less likely to catch a disease. If you and others are educated and content, the crime rate declines, and that improves my standard of living. By the wealth idea, one man is poor because another man is rich; by a standard of living, one man is poor because another is poor.

It is no wonder, then, that in the late twentieth century, when, as never before, we are dominated by concern for our standard of living, we should give a central place to education. For the education of my neighbors, we assume, improves my human environment, and hence raises my standard of living. To build a public school may not increase my wealth; it is likely to affect my standard of living. The 1954 integration decision of the Supreme Court (Brown v. Board of Education of Topeka) was based on the assumption that a standard of living is pervasive, reciprocal, and communal. It was not enough that Negroes should have access to similar instruction, or to private instruction. Equality in a standard-of-living society meant the right to be educated together with and in the presence of other Americans. The opportunities that had historically been given to white Americans could themselves benefit the Negro—but only if he received his education along with them, and in their presence.

Although standard of living is somehow a measure, and a public measure, it is necessarily vague. Wealth can be specifically and precisely defined and weighed, but standard of living has no boundaries. It includes everything in our experience—the production and distribution systems that help us acquire material goods, the climate, the air we breathe, the water we drink, our access to the woods, the richness of our thoughts, the sensitivity of our feelings, and our peace of mind.

The very notion of standard of living is cosmopolitan and universalizing. Just as the Old World mercantilist idea of wealth (essentially treasure) drove others toward autarky and competition among nations, so the American idea of standard of living drives us toward cooperation and world community. In the long run, our ability to raise our American standard of living will depend on our ability to remove the menaces to our health and peace of body and mind, which come from the dissatisfactions and lack of satisfactions of men anywhere.

In the eighteenth century, nations believing the mercantilist dogma organized their laws and commerce to prevent other nations from acquiring their know-how. Jefferson had to smuggle rice seeds out of France and Italy. The plans for the first weaving machines in the United States had to be illegally exported from England; it was unlawful for many kinds of skilled workmen to leave the country. By contrast, in the twentieth century the Marshall Plan, Point IV, and other aid programs express our belief that our peace and prosperity may depend on our ability to raise the standard of living of others. What could more dramatically express our belief in the communal character of material well-being?

It is misleading, then, to think of "conspicuous consumption" as a pathological expression of the oddities of the rich or the perverse. In the United States in the mid-twentieth century nearly all consumption has become conspicuous. Private consumption is the phenomenon of wealth societies. Ours is a standard-of-living society. How otherwise than by public consumption can one signal his membership in Consumption Communities? We learn how to consume, how to join these communities, by seeing how others consume. Advertisers seek to inform us of Consumption Communities and to persuade us to join them. Each of us informs other consumers of our loyalty to these Consumption Communities simply by showing how we consume. The sharing experience that comes to groups of us because we consume the same brands, comes to all of us because we share a standard of living.

A NEW FELLOWSHIP OF CONSUMPTION

To speak of American "materialism" is, then, both an understatement and a misstatement. The material goods that historically have been the symbols which elsewhere separated men from one another have become, under American conditions, symbols which hold men together. From the moment of our rising in the morning, the breakfast food we eat, the coffee we drink, the automobile we drive to work—all these and nearly all the things we consume become thin, but not negligible, bonds with thousands of other Americans.

In our society, then, when the impoverished cannot afford to consume like others they are not merely deprived —they are excluded. They become outsiders because they are not linked by bonds that unite other Americans.

Consumption Communities, both by their strengths and by their weaknesses, reveal to us peculiar features of American life in our time. Older forms of community—of family, of nation, and of religion—of course still continue to bind men together. But the distinctive twentieth-century form of community evolved in modern America is the Consumption Community—measured and displayed in a standard of living.

Modern American life, if we count Consumption Communities among its permanent features, is characterized by new communities far more numerous and far less intense than those of earlier ages. Many—even most—are communities of men and women not in one another's presence. They are diffused and dispersed over the country. Of course these communities are milder, less exclusive and less intense than those that held men together in an early New England Puritan village or in a westward-moving wagon train.

But the communities of Winston smokers and Mustang drivers—or, more broadly, of cigarette smokers and car owners—are nonetheless communities. Their members recognize one another, and share their illusions, hopes, and disappointments. These illusions, hopes, and disappointments are, to be sure, trivial beside those of the Visible Saints of the Massachusetts Bay Colony. But while the seventeenth-century New Englanders were members of only a few communities, the twentieth-century American is a member of countless communities.

The modern American is tied—by the thinnest of threads and by the most volatile, switchable loyalties—to thousands of other Americans by nearly everything he eats or drinks, or wears, or reads, or uses. Old-fashioned political communities and religious communities themselves now become only two among many new, but once unimagined, fellowships. We are held to other men, not only by a few iron bonds, but by countless gossamer webs tying together the trivia of our lives every day.

III

FROM CHARITY
TO PHILANTHROPY

If you are an American interested in education and public institutions and you travel about France today, you find something strangely missing from the landscape. In Paris, of course, you find a host of sites and buildings serving public purposes—from the Champs Élysées, the Place de la Concorde, the Louvre, the Tuilleries, the Petit Palais, the Grand Palais, and the Invalides, to the Collège de France, the Académie, and the Sorbonne. All over the country, of course, you see mairies and parish churches and cathedrals. Along the Loire, on the Côte d'Azure, or scattered elsewhere, splendid chateaux and country estates are monuments to private grandeur, past and present. You are apt to feel puzzled, a bit lost and disoriented, simply because what you see there, like much else in Europe, is classifiable with an unfamiliar neatness. The sites and buildings are, with few exceptions, either public or private. They are monuments of the wealth and power, *either* of individuals *or* of the state. The University of Paris (and there is only one university in

Paris) is an organ of the Ministry of Education; the Louvre and the Bibliothèque Nationale are the responsibility of the minister of culture; the schools are run by the national government. Even the most imposing religious monuments— Notre Dame, Chartres, and Mont-Saint-Michel, for example —are essentially public, for they have been supported by taxation. The French church has enjoyed privileges which (despite the freedom of religion) have amounted to making it an organ of the state. If you are not in a private building, you are in an institution created and supported and controlled by the government.

In a great American city, by contrast, many—even most —of the prominent public buildings and institutions are of a quite different character. They do not fall into either of these sharply separated classes. Strictly speaking, they are not private, nor are they run by the government. They are a third species, which in many important respects is peculiarly American. They have many unique characteristics and a spirit all their own. They are monuments to what in the Old World was familiar neither as private charity nor as governmental munificence. They are monuments to community. They originate in the community, depend on the community, are developed by the community, serve the community, and rise or fall with the community.

They are such familiar features of our American landscape that we can easily forget, if we have ever noticed, that they are in many ways a peculiar American growth—peculiar both in their character and in their luxuriance, in what has made them grow and in what keeps them alive and flourishing. I need hardly remind you of such prominent features of Chicago life as the Art Institute, the Chicago Museum of Natural History (sometimes called the Field Museum), the Shedd Aquarium, the Adler Planetarium, the Museum of Science and Industry (commonly called the Rosenwald Museum), and The University of Chicago (founded by John D. Rockefeller). Each of these—in fact, nearly all the major philanthropic, educational, and public-serving institutions of the city (with some conspicuous exceptions)—was founded and is sustained voluntarily by members of the community. One finds comparable institutions in every other American city. Of course, there are numerous hospitals, universities, and other enterprises supported by our government; but these are far more often the creatures of local or state than of the national government. Scattered examples of community institutions of this type are not unique to the United States. Something like them—some of the Oxford and Cambridge colleges, for example—existed even before the New World was settled by Europeans. In one form or another a few such institutions are found today probably in every country in the world, except in Communist countries, where the autonomous public spirit is prohibited. But in extent, power, influence, and vitality our community institutions are a peculiarly American phenomenon.

Here in the United States, even some of our institutions ostensibly run by one or another of our governments are in fact community institutions in a sense in which they are not elsewhere in the world. Take, for example, our "public" schools. In the great nations of western Europe, the schools which are supported by the general citizenry and which anyone can attend free of charge are run not by separate communities through school boards but from the center by the national government headquartered, say, in Paris or in Rome. It was once a familiar boast of the French minister of education that he could look at his watch at any moment during the day and tell you exactly what was being taught in every classroom in the country. Nothing is more astonishing to a European than to be told that in the United States we have no corresponding official and that, except for a few constitutional safeguards (for example, of freedom of religion, or of free entry to public facilities, regardless of race), the conduct of our public instruction is decentralized. It is in local community hands.

ORIGINS OF AN AMERICAN IDEA OF COMMUNITY: AN OLD ANTITHESIS DISSOLVED

This notion of community is one of the most characteristic, one of the most important, yet one of the least noticed American contributions to modern life. From one point of view it is simply another example of how the time-honored distinctions and sharp antitheses of European life became blurred, befogged, and softened in America. The familiar theme of recent European politics is the antithesis "The Man versus the State," which had already begun to dominate Old World thought even before Herbert Spencer published his book under that title in 1884. Other expressions of this way of thinking were the antitheses "Individualism versus Socialism" and "Laissez Faire versus Collectivism," and there have been many others. This set of polar contrasts has framed much of European public debate. Even in England, where the brittle oppositions of Continental politics tend to be softened by good humor and common sense, they have dominated the political vocabulary. The best general history of English legislation in the nineteenth century—A. V. Dicey's *Law and Opinion*—tells the whole story as a movement from "individualism" to "collectivism."

Meanwhile, in the United States the political vocabulary, by which I mean the vocabulary of debate and not of vituperation, has been different. Despite the extravagant optimism expressed by Marx and Engels that the so-called working masses would be more resentful in the United States than elsewhere, that they would be more revolutionary and more socialistic, still American socialism as an organized articulate movement has made very little headway. The fact is pretty obvious. Socialist parties here have had even less success than our other minor political parties. For example, even during what some textbooks call "The Golden Age of American Socialism," in the first decade of this century, the Socialists were not able to elect more than two Congressional representatives. The only interesting question about socialism in the United States was put by the German economist Werner Sombart in the title of his book, *Why Is There No Socialism in the United States?* The most popular explanation is summed up in Sombart's own observation that "on the reefs of roast beef and apple pie socialistic Utopias of every sort are sent to their doom."

There is another, or rather, additional, explanation, which so far as I know has not yet been seriously proposed but which may help us understand much that is distinctive about our political life and about our whole culture, including the forms given to the philanthropic spirit in America. Yet it is very simple and obvious: the American idea and institution of community.

We have been misled into thinking that the terms of the European debate force us too into a choice between the two terms, "individualism" and "socialism." This false choice inevitably leads us to put ourselves, or to think we can put ourselves, in the camp of "individualism." It is significant that the first use of "individualism" in the English language recorded by the *Oxford English Dictionary* is in Henry Reeve's translation (1840) of Tocqueville's *Democracy in America*. Reeve apologizes for taking the word directly from the French. Tocqueville used the word to describe what he thought was an American way of feeling; but here his misunderstanding of American life was peculiarly

French, or, rather, Old Worldly, for he used "individualism" as a term of half-reproach, describing it as "of democratic origin, and it threatens to spread in the same ratio as the equality of conditions." With the eye of a perceptive but short-term traveler, he was understandably baffled by the attitude of Americans toward the activities of their governments.

After Tocqueville, the term "individualism," like "socialism," had very little vogue in America for most of the nineteenth century. Walt Whitman vaunted the "individual," but he was no man of doctrine. The best known use of the word "individualism" in recent American history was by Herbert Hoover in a campaign speech in New York (October 22, 1928), when he offered it as half of the familiar European antithesis: "We were challenged with a peacetime choice between the American system of rugged individualism and a European philosophy of diametrically opposed doctrines—doctrines of paternalism and state socialism."

Just as the antitheses "The Man versus the State" and "Individualism versus Socialism" had little relevance in America, so too the word "individualism" would be a misleading slogan if identified with an American Way of Life. Of course Americans had an unprecedented opportunity to discover their individuality, and of course many Americans have been preoccupied with their own private interests even in conflict with those of the community. But egotism, in the sense of unalloyed selfishness, has probably played no greater role in American history than elsewhere. To emphasize this aspect of American life is simply to try to import one of the Siamese twins of modern European politics. Yet to us the one is no more relevant than the other. What is instead peculiar to our way of thinking and feeling is the idea of community.

In Origin, American Communities Were Voluntary:
Communities Arose Before Governments

In western Europe, with insignificant exceptions, men found themselves wherever they were in the nineteenth century because they were born there. The act of choice, of consciously choosing their particular community, had been made, if ever, only by remote ancestors—the contemporaries of Beowulf, William the Conqueror, Siegfried, or Aeneas. On the other hand, because we were an immigrant nation, everybody here, except the Indians and the Negroes and those others who had been forcibly transported, was here because he or a recent ancestor (a father, grandfather, or great-grandfather) had chosen this place. The sense of community was inevitably more vivid and more personal because, for so many in the community, living here had been an act of choice.

In crowded, pre-empted Europe, with its no-trespassing signs all over the place, the control of governments, by the nineteenth century or even before, covered the map. The decisive contrasting fact, not sufficiently noticed, is that in America, even in modern times, *communities* existed before governments were here to care for public needs. There were many groups of people with a common sense of purpose and a feeling of duty to one another before there were political institutions forcing them to perform their duties. A classic example is the Pilgrims, who landed at Plymouth in November, 1620. Of course, they were held together by a strong sense of common purpose. But since they were landing in an unexpected place—they had intended to land in Virginia and not in New England—they were a community without government. While still on board the *Mayflower,* they were frightened by the boast of their few unruly members who threatened to take advantage of this fact as soon as they touched land. So by the Mayflower Compact they set up a new government. The Pilgrim community thus had preceded the government of Plymouth.

This order of events was repeated again and again in American history. Groups moving westward from New England and other parts of the Atlantic seaboard organized themselves into communities in order to conquer the great distances, to help one another drag their wagons uphill, to protect one another from Indians, and for a hundred other co-operative purposes. They knew they were moving into open spaces where jurisdiction was uncertain or nonexistent. Or take the remote mining towns, founded here and there in what is now Colorado, California, Montana, or Nevada—places where men knew that their silver or golden objects could not be secured unless they managed to stay alive and preserve their property. In all these places men who were already a community formed do-it-yourself governments. Communities preceded governments.

Not least important was this phenomenon in the new western cities. Chicago was to be the greatest, but there were others, like Cincinnati, Kansas City, Omaha, and Denver, which had become flourishing communities before they had well-established, elaborate governments.

This simple American order of experience was to have deep and widespread effects on American thinking about society, government, and the responsibilities of the individual. While Europe was everywhere cluttered with obsolete political machinery, in America *purposes* usually preceded machinery. In Europe it was more usual for the voluntary activities of groups to grow up in the interstices of ancient government agencies. In America more often the voluntary collaborative activities of members of the community were there first, and it was government that came into the interstices. Thus, while Americans acquired a wholesome respect for the force of the community organized into governments, they tended to feel toward it neither awe, nor reverence, nor terror. The scrupulous faithfulness with which most Americans pay most of their taxes (even their income taxes!) continually astonishes continental Europeans. This is only another vivid reminder that Americans tend to think of government as their servant and not their master. While we have less faith in government and expect less of it, we also have less suspicion of it.

The Ideal of Maximal Community

Seldom have a people been more anxious than Americans have been to share their common purposes. We are desperately earnest to make our community include as much as possible of our daily life. This has sometimes been ridiculed in such phrases as "Babbittry" or "the organization man," but it goes deeper than has been suspected and reaches far back in our history. In our country, unlike France, for example, if you are somebody's business associate, you are expected also to be his golf partner, his friend, and to share his general religious beliefs, his political ideals, and his standard of living.

In the seventeenth century the American Puritans began with an encompassing, we might say a "totalitarian," concept of community. Nowadays, fortunately, we only seldom require people to subscribe formally to explicit beliefs; but we still expect people to act and feel as if they believed the same thing. To pass for a religious person in the United States, it is less important that you be able to define sharply what you believe than that you be able, however vaguely, to share the equally vague religiosity of others. Our political faith is much the same. It is less important for an American public man to have clearly defined political principles (he may seem dangerous if he does) than for him to share the vague political beliefs of as many as possible of his fellow-citizens. Thus, although we proclaim ourselves to be a religious nation by the word "God" on our coins and (by Act of Congress) in our Pledge of Allegiance, it is unlawful to express or avow in our public schools any specific religious sentiments to which everybody else could not agree. Our political parties must have platforms; but no party would get far unless its platform was as much as possible like that of the other party.

A sometimes discomfiting aspect of our ideal of maximal community is the proverbial American lack of privacy. We insist that public servants—or even public figures—share their private lives with us. Not the walled garden, but the front porch, the open lawn, and the golf course are the scenes of the so-called private lives of our public men.

The Quick-Grown, Fluid Community: The Booster Spirit

In nineteenth-century England a number of cities like London, Birmingham, and Manchester grew with unprecedented rapidity. But this speed was slow compared to the contemporary growth of many American cities, which became metropolises almost before geographers had located them on their maps. The population of Illinois, for example, more than quadrupled between 1810 and 1820, more than trebled between 1820 and 1830, and again between 1830 and 1840. The city of Chicago (then Fort Dearborn), which around 1830 counted a hundred people, by 1890 had passed the million mark. Though it had taken a million years for mankind to produce its first city of a million inhabitants, Americans—or perhaps we should say Chicagoans—accomplished this gargantuan feat within a single lifetime.

Similar phenomena occurred not only in Chicago but in dozens of other places—in Omaha, Cincinnati, Denver, Kansas City, St. Louis, and Dallas, to mention only a few.

Such fantastic growth itself fostered a naïve pride in community, for men literally grew up with their towns. From this simple fact came a much maligned but peculiarly American product: the Booster Spirit. The spirit which had grown in the nineteenth century was pretty conscious of itself by about 1900 when the word "booster" was invented. In cities of explosive growth, group needs were urgent and rapidly changing. Sewage disposal, water supply, sidewalks, parks, harbor facilities, and a thousand other common needs at first depended on the desires, the willingness, and the good will of individuals. Could people who had very little governmental machinery do these things for themselves and their neighbors? Could they rapidly change the scale and the ends of their thinking about their town? Were they willing? By saying "Yes," they proved that they were a community.

Hardly less remarkable than this sudden intensity of community feeling in upstart cities was the fluidity of the population and the readiness with which people came and went. During a single day in the summer of 1857, thirty-four hundred immigrants arrived in Chicago on the Michigan Central Railroad alone. People came not only from the eastern and southern United States but from Ireland, Germany, and Scandinavia, and, very soon, too, from Poland, Italy, China, and other remote places. People who came so readily sometimes also left soon and in large numbers. Such cities flourished partly because they were distribution points—spigots from which people poured into the sponge-like hinterland.

Thus was nourished the Booster Spirit, distinctively American not only in intensity and volubleness but in the readiness with which it could be detached from one community and attached to another. Booster loyalties grew rapidly; yet while they lasted, they seemed to have an oaklike solidity. Here today and there tomorrow. Chicago today; tomorrow Omaha, Denver, or Tulsa. "But while I'm here, I'm with you 150 per cent." "We'll outgrow and outshine all the rest!" Never was a loyalty more fervent, more enthusiastic, more noisy—or more transferable. This was the voluntary, competitive spirit. It was illustrated in people like Dr. Daniel Drake (1785–1852), who was born in New Jersey, migrated to Kentucky, and became an early booster of Cincinnati, publishing in 1815 the first influential promotional tract for the city. But he spent much of his later life in Lexington and Louisville, where the prospects for his profession looked better.

How natural that we should become a nation of "joiners" when—provided one was not a Negro or a member of certain other marked minorities—one could join or leave his community at will. And much of the time one was likely to be considering moving to other still more attractive communities.

Everywhere personal and community prosperity were intermixed in many obvious ways. Community meant common*wealth*. Each person who came into town was one more customer, one more client, one more patient—in short, another potential booster. His mere presence increased the value of real estate and the business possibilities for everyone. To build Chicago, then, was to build my own fortune. By building my fortune, I built Chicago. We can detect this same interfusion of ideas in mid-twentieth-century when Charles Wilson says, "What's good for General Motors is good for the country" and when Walter Reuther replies by saying, "What's good for America is good for the Labor Movement."

The keynote of all this was *community*. American history

had helped empty the word of its connotations of selfless-ness. Notice how irrelevant were the antitheses of "Individ-ualism" versus "Socialism," "The Man" versus "The State." Governments here were not the transformed instruments of hereditary power. American businessmen were eager and ingenious at finding ways for federal, state, or local govern-ment to serve their enterprises—whether they were New England shippers, western lumbermen, transcontinental railroad-builders, manufacturers, or simple farmers or mer-chants. Of course, this was not because they were socialists but rather because, starting from the fact of community, they could not help seeing all agencies of government as ad-ditional forms through which specific community purposes could be served.

FROM CONSCIENCE TO COMMUNITY

There are few better illustrations of this central concept—perhaps it might better be called a sentiment—in American life than the history of American philanthropy. And there has been no more effective exponent of the community spirit in philanthropy than Julius Rosenwald, the centennial of whose birth was celebrated on October 15, 1962. I will not try to tell the story of Rosenwald's philanthropies. I will, rather, describe some of the distinctiveness of certain Amer-ican developments and show how Julius Rosenwald partici-pated in them.

Philanthropy or charity throughout much of European history has been a predominantly private virtue. In most of western Europe the national states and their organs were elaborated before the needs of modern industrial society came into being. The state and its organs had therefore pre-empted most of the areas of public benevolence, improve-ment, education, and progress even before the appearance of the great fortunes which modern industry made possible. The creators of the modern state—for example, Queen Elizabeth I in England, Napoleon in France, and Bismarck in Germany—developed arms of the state to do more and more jobs of public service, public enrichment, public enlightenment, and cultural and scientific progress. The charitable spirit was a kind of residuum; it inevitably tended to become the spirit of almsgiving. Of course, everybody was required to contribute by taxes or gifts to state or church institutions. But because the state—and its ancient partner, the church—had taken over the business of wholesale philanthropy, the independent charities of wealthy men were generally left to alleviating the distress of the particular individuals whom they noticed.

By the nineteenth century in France or Italy—even in England—it was by no means easy, though one had the means and the desire, to found a new university (the legislature might not charter it; it might confuse or compete against the state-organized system; it might become a center of "revolutionary" or of "reactionary" ideology; etc.), a new museum, or a new research institute. The right to establish new institutions, like the right to bear arms, was jealously guarded by the sovereign, which, of course, usually meant the single national government at the center.

Meanwhile Christian teachings had long exalted the spirit of charity and the practice of almsgiving. "If thou wilt be perfect, go and sell that thou hast, and give to the poor, and thou shalt have treasure in heaven: and come and follow me. . . . Verily I say unto you, That a rich man shall hardly enter into the kingdom of heaven." (Matt. 19:21–23) "Knowledge puffeth up, but charity edifieth." (I Cor. 8:1) "And now abideth faith, hope, charity, these three; but the greatest of these is charity." (I Cor. 13:13) Charity ennobled the giver; it was more blessed to give than to receive.

The first characteristic of the traditional charitable spirit, then, was that it was *private* and *personal*. This fact has made difficulties for scholars trying to chronicle philanthropy, especially outside the United States. Donors have often been reluctant to make known the size (whether because of the smallness or the largeness) of their donations. They have sometimes feared that signs of their wealth might bring down on them a host of the poor, confiscatory demands from the tax farmer, or jealousy from the sovereign. For more reasons than one, therefore, charity, which was a salve for the conscience, became an innermost corner of consciousness, a sanctum of privacy. A man's charities were a matter between him and his God. Church and conscience might be intermediaries, but the community did not belong in the picture.

Second, the traditional charitable spirit was perpetual, unchanging, and, even in a certain sense, rigid. "The poor," said Jesus, "ye always have with you." (John 12:8) The almsgiver was less likely to be trying to solve a problem of this world than to be earning his right to enter into the next. There hardly seemed to be any problem of means or of purpose. Since it was always a greater virtue to give than to receive, the goodness of charity came more from the motive of the giver than from the effect of the gift. Only a hypocrite, a proud man, or one impure of heart would hesitate while he chose among the objects of the gift.

The philanthropic spirit, as it has developed, changed, flourished, and become peculiarly institutionalized in America, has been very different. In some respects it has even been opposed to these two characteristics of the time-honored virtue. Here, again, the dominant note, the pervading spirit, the peculiar characteristic, has been a preoccupation with community. This transformation of the charitable spirit has been expressed in at least three peculiarly American emphases.

Community Enrichment: The Purposes of Philanthropy

The focus of American philanthropy has shifted from the giver to the receiver, from the salving of souls to the solving of problems, from conscience to community. No one better expressed this spirit than Julius Rosenwald, when he said:

> In the first place "philanthropy" is a sickening word. It is generally looked upon as helping a man who hasn't a cent in the world. That sort of thing hardly interests me. I do not like the "sob stuff" philanthropy. What I want to do is to try to cure the things that seem to be wrong. I do not underestimate the value of helping the underdog. That, however, is not my chief concern but rather the operation of cause and effect. I try to do the thing that will aid groups and masses rather than individuals.

This view, which we should probably call (in William James's phrase) "tough-minded" rather than hardhearted, has long dominated what has been the peculiarly American charitable spirit.

The patron saint of American philanthropy is not Dorothea Dix or any other saintly person but rather Benjamin Franklin, the man with a business sense and an eye on his community. For Franklin, doing good was not a private act between bountiful giver and grateful receiver; it was a prudent social act. A wise act of philanthropy would sooner or later benefit the giver along with all other members of the community. While living in Philadelphia, Franklin developed philanthropic enterprises which included projects for establishing a city police, for the paving and the better cleaning and lighting of city streets, for a circulating library, for the American Philosophical Society for Useful Knowledge, for an Academy for the Education of Youth (origin of the University of Pennsylvania), for a debating society, and for a volunteer fire department.

Like Julius Rosenwald, Franklin did not go in for "sob-stuff" philanthropy. Few, if any, of his enterprises were primarily for the immediate relief of distress or misfortune. Notice, also, that in Franklin's mind and in his activities the line between public and private hardly existed. If an activity was required and was not yet performed by a government— by city, state, or nation—he thought it perfectly reasonable that individuals club together to do the job, not only to fill the gap, but also to prod or shame governments into doing their part. A large number, but by no means all, of his activities have been taken over by the municipality of Philadelphia, the state of Pennsylvania, or the federal government. From his point of view the important thing was not whether the job was done by government or by individuals: both governments and individuals were agencies of community. The community was the thing. Notice also that Franklin's opportunity to step into the breach with community enterprises arose in large part because the community was relatively new, because state activities were still sparse—in a word, because the community existed before the government.

Julius Rosenwald was sometimes unable to resist his impulse to help the individual, and he did occasionally obey the almsgiving impulse—most notably during the stock-market crash of October, 1929. He was himself no speculator, yet at the time of the crash he promptly and unhesitatingly supported the initiative of his son, Lessing Rosenwald, and guaranteed the personal stock-market accounts of about three hundred of his employees, thus saving many of these families from financial collapse. His greatest contributions, as we all know, were to the Negro—not so much to the direct relief of destitution among Negroes as to the cause of Negro education. He did this in part by the wise expenditure of over twenty-two million dollars through the Rosenwald Fund alone. He was not the largest philanthropist of this century, but there was none who gave more thought to the purposes and community effect of his gifts. "Viewing the matter in retrospect," Rosenwald observed in 1929, "I can testify that it is nearly always easier to make one million dollars honestly than to dispose of it wisely."

While publicly generous, he was not personally extravagant. The story is told that, when Rosenwald was traveling by Pullman one night between Chicago and New York, another Pullman porter asked the porter of the car in which Rosenwald was sleeping whether he had any interesting passengers. The porter glowed with excitement as he boasted, "I've got Julius Rosenwald!"

After the train arrived in New York, the first porter asked the second again, "How did you make out?"

To which he received the reply, "All right, but I guess Mr. Rosenwald is really more for the race than for the individual."

Community Participation: The Means of Philanthropy

While, as we have just observed, the focus of American philanthropy has shifted from giver to receiver, there has occurred another equally important shift in point of view. The clear lines between the roles of the giver and the receiver, which in the traditional European situation were so distinct, in America became blurred. In an American equalitarian, enterprising, fluid society the ancient contrasts between the bountiful rich and the grateful poor, the benefactor and the beneficiary, on which the almsgiving situation had depended, became obsolete. In America a community—the ultimate beneficiary—was increasingly expected to be its own benefactor. The recipient here (who became more difficult to identify as a member of a fixed social class) was now viewed less as a target of individual generosity than as an integral part of the social capital, an item of community investment.

It is not surprising, then, that the time-honored notion that it is more blessed to give than to receive, like some other ancient fixed axioms of charity, began to be dissolved. When you no longer believe the ancient axiom that "the poor are always with you," a recipient is no longer a member of a permanent social class. So far did we move from the old notion; now the ideal recipient of philanthropy was himself viewed as a potential donor. Just as the value of a charitable gift tended to be judged less by the motive of the giver than by the social effect of the gift, so the suitability of a recipient was judged less by his emotional response —his gratitude or his personal loyalty to a benefactor— than by his own potential contribution to the community. A free citizen who receives assistance is no mere receptacle of benevolence; he prepares himself to become a fountain of benevolence.

By a twist of New World circumstances, by the transformation of the charitable spirit, in the United States it often happened that those who received most from an act of philanthropy were also those who gave most. Julius Rosenwald, and some other characteristically American philanthropists, have viewed this as the ideal philanthropic situation. Take, for example, a scene in Boligee, Alabama, in the winter of 1916–17. This was one of the so-called arousement meetings to raise money from the local Negro community to meet Julius Rosenwald's offer of a matching sum to build a simple schoolhouse. We are fortunate to have an eyewitness account:

> We gathered together in a little old rickety building, without any heat, only from an old rusty stove with the stove pipe protruding out of the window where a pane had been removed for the flue. . . . The farmers had been hard hit that year as the boll weevil had figured very conspicuously in that community, and most of the people were tenants on large plantations. When we reached the scene where the rally was to be staged, the teacher with thirty-five or forty little children had prepared a program which consisted of plantation melodies. . . . They sang with such fervor and devotion, until one could hardly restrain from crying. . . . The patrons and friends were all rural people, and crudely dressed. The women had on home spun dresses and aprons, while the men in the main were dressed in blue overalls. Their boots and shoes were very muddy, as they had to trudge through the mud from three to four miles. . . . When the speaking was over we arranged for the silver offering, and to tell the truth I thought we would do well to collect ten dollars from the audience; but when the Master of Ceremonies, Rev. M. D. Wallace, who had ridden a small mule over the county through the cold and through the rain, organizing the people, began to call the collection the people began to respond. You would have been over-awed with emotion if you could have seen those poor people walking up to the table, emptying their pockets for a school. . . . One old man, who had seen slavery days, with all of his life's earnings in an old greasy sack, slowly drew it from his pocket, and emptied it on the table. I have never seen such a pile of nickels, pennies, dimes, and dollars, etc., in my life. He put thirty-eight dollars on the table, which was his entire savings.

These were the people who would benefit most from the Rosenwald gift, yet they were the people who in proportion to their means were giving most.

Someone with less faith in his fellow men might simply have given the sums outright without asking any matching funds, for the Negroes of Alabama were surely depressed and underprivileged. In a recent previous year, when the state of Alabama had appropriated $2,865,254 for public education, only $357,585, or less than 15 per cent, went to Negro schools. This despite the fact that Negroes made up about half the population of the state. Rosenwald had faith in the Negroes of Alabama—not only in their potentiality but, still more important, in their present determination and their ability to help themselves.

By the time of his death, Rosenwald had contributed to the construction of 5,357 public schools, shops, and teachers' homes in 883 counties of fifteen southern states at a total cost of $28,408,520. Julius Rosenwald's personal contribution was monumental: $4,366,519. But a fact of which he would have been still prouder was that his contribution had induced others to contribute still more. While his contribution amounted to 15 per cent of the whole, the Negroes themselves had given $4,725,871, or 17 per cent. Local white friends had contributed $1,211,975, or 4 per cent. And tax funds in these communities had contributed $18,104,115, or 64 per cent.

In his attitude Rosenwald was not alone. Leading American philanthropists of his day shared his view. Carnegie would not give a library building without assurance that the community would invest heavily in its support. An obvious but most important common characteristic of the greatest American philanthropic enterprises of the nineteenth and early twentieth centuries in this country—of Carnegie's libraries, museums, and music halls; of the universities endowed by Vanderbilt, Cornell, Stanford, and Rockefeller; of the art galleries and institutes aided by Cooper, Peabody, and Mellon—was that they were voluntary organizations. No one would be helped by them unless the person himself was willing to make an effort to help himself. The passive beneficiary had no place in this scheme. He benefited most from a library who worked most there. "The best means of benefiting the community," said Carnegie, "is to place within its reach the ladders upon which the aspiring can rise." Thus the struggle for equal educational opportunities for everybody everywhere is the most characteristically American and the most fruitful form of philanthropy.

When philanthropy ceases to be a matter only between a man and his God, when the community enters, then anonymity loses much of its blessedness. For the community has a right to know, and can profit from knowing. Although Julius Rosenwald again and again refused his permission to let institutions be named after him (for example, the Museum of Science and Industry), and repeatedly refused incidental honors like honorary degrees, he was opposed to anonymous giving. Simply because he believed that one of the purposes of giving was to stimulate others to give, Rosenwald believed that secrecy and inactivity were likely to go together and to explain each other.

Adaptation to Community: The Flexibility of Philanthropy

Faith, hope, and charity were as changeless as God or human nature, but philanthropy must change with its community. American philanthropists were citizens of fast-growing cities with shifting populations, novel enterprises, and a speedy obsolescence of social problems as of everything else. To do their job, they had to keep their eyes open and their feet on the ground. They had to be alert to new needs which required new investments by everybody in a progressive community.

Julius Rosenwald, who had grown up with the West and with Chicago, was well aware of all this. He warned vain men against seeking immortality by attaching their names to institutions; he reminded them of Nesselrode, "who lived a diplomat, but is immortal as a pudding."

Rosenwald never tired of pointing to the dangers of rigid philanthropy, of gifts in perpetuity for unchanging purposes, which might become a burden rather than a blessing. He recalled the case of the Brian Mullanphy Fund, established in 1851 for "worthy and distressed travelers and emigrants passing through St. Louis to settle for a home in the West"—a fund which, for lack of beneficiaries even before Rosenwald's time, totaled a million dollars. Or the fund established by John Edgar Thompson, once president of the Pennsylvania Railroad, who gave two million dollars for the benefit of daughters of railroad workers whose lives were accidentally lost in the service of the company. Because of the decline in railway accidents, the fund was virtually without a purpose in 1930; and the decline of railways would make it even more difficult for Mr. Thompson's purpose to be served in later years. Or there was the benefactor of Bryn Mawr College who, in days before the weight-losing fad, left a fund to provide a baked potato for each young lady there at every meal.

His favorite example, and one still very relevant, was the orphan asylum. "Orphan asylums," Rosenwald remarked in 1929, "began to disappear about the time the old-fashioned wall telephone went out." Yet millions had been accumulating for orphan asylums; at that date the Hershey endowment for these purposes alone totaled over forty million dollars. But ideas had changed. Already in 1929, it was generally believed that other ways of helping orphans, for example, placing them in foster homes, were far preferable.

Julius Rosenwald's long experience as a Trustee of The University of Chicago further convinced him, as he observed on numerous occasions, of the unwisdom of philanthropic gifts narrowly limited. It takes courage for a man to crusade for his ideas and to stake his life and fortune on them; it takes still greater courage for a man to stake his life and fortune on a belief that his ideas will become obsolete.

Perhaps Julius Rosenwald's leading contribution to our thinking about philanthropy was his insistence on the need for flexibility in American philanthropic institutions. In his widely read article, "Principles of Public Giving" (*Atlantic Monthly*, May, 1929), and its sequel, "The Trend Away from Perpetuities" (*Atlantic Monthly*, December, 1930), he championed lifetime, rather than testamentary, giving and urged other ways of allowing each generation to face its own problems. He believed in applying to charity the Jeffersonian axiom that the earth belongs to the living. The Rosenwald Fund, which was probably one of the most successful philanthropic enterprises of this or any other century, was set up with the express provision, which Rosenwald wrote into the gift, that both the income and all the principal be spent within twenty-five years of Rosenwald's death. Rosenwald died in 1932, and the Fund, under able direction, lived up to this requirement, terminating its work in 1948.

Since Julius Rosenwald's day, two new kinds of problems in the application of the American community idea to philanthropic institutions have become acute. The first has arisen from the vast foundations which appeared in the first decades of our century. They are something new under the sun. With the expansion of the American economy, older forms of philanthropy proved inadequate to distribute the enormous sums accumulated by men of wealth. A series of foundations was then established; some of the more important were The Rockefeller Institute for Medical Research (1901), The General Education Board (1902), The Carnegie Foundation for the Advancement of Teaching (1905), The Milbank Memorial Fund (1905), The Russell Sage Foundation (1907), The Carnegie Corporation of New York (1911), and The Rockefeller Foundation (1913). These differed from earlier philanthropic enterprises not only in their number and in the size of their capital but in the nature of their purposes and in the discretion allowed their trustees. Few, if any, of these donors now made the mistake of Brian Mullanphy, who thought that wagon trains would always be coming through St. Louis. For the first time the community's largest accumulations of philanthropic wealth were theoretically, at least, available for any, including the vaguest, purpose, such as the advancement of knowledge and human welfare.

The Income Tax Amendment to the Constitution (the 16th), which became law in 1913, in the long run had the unexpected effect of enlarging the resources of these gargantuan general-purpose philanthropic funds. As early as the 1930's it was widely recognized that a person in the higher-income brackets, with expert advice, could make large contributions with little sacrifice of spendable income and often to his own advantage in other ways. Capital-gains tax could be avoided by giving appreciated stock to a foundation, and yet, as a trustee, the donor could continue to vote the stock. There were many ways also in which foundations could help donors avoid gift and estate taxes. In the 1940's all these factors became still more important. A revision of the Revenue Code in 1950 was necessary to deal with the abuses of foundations for private purposes. But the tax benefits remained so great as to continue to encourage the growth of foundations. By the mid-1950's the number of ostensibly philanthropic foundations was at least five thousand and, by some calculations, had reached seventy-five hundred. The *Foundation Directory* is now a thick volume.

The most spectacular, and in many respects the most characteristic, of the foundations was the Ford Foundation. It had been organized in 1936, concentrating on local and family affairs until after the death of Henry Ford in 1947, and then it became active nationally in the 1950's. At that time it possessed 90 per cent of the stock of one of the largest corporations in the country. The market value of its assets in the early 1960's was somewhere around two and a half billion dollars, amounting to about one-third of the combined assets of all foundations. Even as early as 1954 its annual appropriations came to between a fourth and a fifth of total foundation spending.

While in many respects these foundations were squarely in the American tradition which I have described, they faced new problems and themselves created some. Many of these are not unrelated to the dangers against which Julius Rosenwald warned, although they arise from some opposite causes. The perpetuities, the rigidities, and the bureaucracies against which Rosenwald inveighed were in charities whose purposes were too specific and hence likely to become obsolete. But the foundations which dominate the scene nowadays are extremely general in their purpose. The public dangers which arise from them come precisely from the fact that there is no prospect that they will ever become obsolete. The Ford Foundation's purpose is to serve the public welfare.

Spontaneity, drift, fluidity, and competition among American institutions have given our culture much of its vitality. Some of the dangers which come from the new large foundations spring from the very vagueness and generality of their purposes as well as from their sheer size. They have already become powerful, independent, self-perpetuating institutions. They are in the wholesale—some might say the "mail-order"—philanthropy business. Instead of encouraging latent energies in the community, they are naturally tempted to initiate projects; and the more spectacular and more novel are often most attractive from a public relations point of view. They show few signs of that self-liquidating tendency that Rosenwald rightly insisted to be a feature of a healthy foundation.

The entry into our language of certain phrases is a clue to the changing spirit of our large-scale philanthropy and to the new dangers. We all have heard of the "foundation executive"—a person who makes his living from administering philanthropy, from inventing, developing, and publicizing worthy projects. He is often a refugee from academic life; he is seldom underpaid (at least by academic standards); ideally, he is a person of driving energy, of aggressive organizing power, and of all the affable virtues. He is a new breed of the American college president, another expert on things in general, who has the new advantage of being able to exert his affability on the disbursement rather than on the collection of funds. But some might ask whether one such breed is not enough and perhaps all that our culture can stand. Amusement is sometimes expressed by professors when they find themselves solemnly presenting their appeals for support of their research to foundation officials who left university life precisely because they were unable to produce research which satisfied these very same professors.

Another telltale phrase which has entered our vocabulary is the so-called "foundation project." Generally speaking, a foundation project must be collaborative; it must have defined and predictable results; it must be noncontroversial;

and yet it must have some popular interest. The fact that we in academic life know what kind of project will appeal or will not appeal to the foundations is one of the worst things that can be said about them. Generally speaking, instead of being an incentive to the initiative of individuals or communities, our largest foundations have tended to foster (as, indeed, they created) the vogue for concocted projects cast in the foundation mold. Thus foundations become freezing agents in the world of scholarship and of community projects. Their proper role is as catalyst.

An even larger new problem has arisen in the mid-twentieth century from our efforts to apply our philanthropic spirit abroad. At least since the Marshall Plan (or European Recovery Plan, which between 1948 and 1951 helped western European countries bolster their economies by gifts and loans to the amount of 12.5 billion dollars), and the "Point Four" program, outlined by President Truman in his Inaugural Address of January 20, 1949, followed by large programs under the succeeding Presidents of both parties, the role of philanthropist-to-the-world (or to the free, or potentially free, world) has been irrevocably assumed by the United States.

Two dangers lie in our new role, seen in the perspective of our peculiar national history. The first is that—in our enthusiasm to do good, in our optimism, our desire to encompass the world in our community, and to put the best light on everything we do—we may confuse ourselves into assuming that charity and self-interest are always necessarily consistent. In this confusion we not only fail to see the clear dictates of our national self-interest but becloud our purer acts of charity with suspicions of Machiavellism.

The second danger here arises from the peculiar character of American life, in which, as I have said, the idea of community has been central. In the United States our distinctive philanthropic institutions have been neither wholly public nor wholly private; they have been acts of community, depending for their success and their meaning on the triple ideas of community enrichment, community participation, and adaptation to community. If philanthropy has arisen in America out of our poignant and pressing sense of community, does it follow that elsewhere in the world the sense of community itself can arise merely or even mainly from outside acts of philanthropy?

Our phenomenal success and our phenomenal energies in developing philanthropic institutions for our own community may mislead us into overlooking how much that success has depended on the pre-existence here of a sense of community. From being a single aspect of American domestic institutions, philanthropy—the charitable spirit—in its transformed American shapes has become the leading feature of our relation to the world. Not merely the prosperity but the very survival of the United States may now depend on our ability to see where charity ends and where national self-interest begins—on our ability, in Julius Rosenwald's words, not to be overwhelmed by "the 'sob-stuff' philanthropy," but to look hard at "the operation of cause and effect" and to "try to cure the things that seem to be wrong." This will depend not only on whether we can train a few thousand Peace Corpsmen or a few tens of thousands of administrators of foreign aid but on whether we can look unashamedly (as Rosenwald did) at the limits of our capacity to help others and on whether we can—even at some risk to ourselves—share Rosenwald's faith in the ability of other peoples and future generations to solve their own problems.

TWO

☆ ☆

IV

THE PERILS OF
INDWELLING LAW

Of all terms used by social scientists today, "Law" and "Society" are perhaps the most vaguely interrelated. In some sense or other law is a creature of society, and society is a creature of law. We generally think of a law-breaker as a person who is anti-social. We cannot contribute to the improvement of our laws without at the same time contributing to the improvement of society. On the other hand, a person can be anti-social without being a lawbreaker; and a person is not always serving his society by obeying its laws.

"Society" is in some ways a much larger term than "Law." Every society includes a system of law, yet "Law" is somehow more durable, more chronologically extensive. "Roman Society" calls to mind the way men lived at some particular time. But "Roman Law" suggests ways of living that extended over generations. "Society" extends primarily in space; "Law" primarily in time. The relations between "Law" and "Society" then must have something to do with the relations between the peculiar needs and habits of men in some particular place at a given time, and the persistent practices of a large group of men over generations.

I wish to focus not on the "real" relationship between a Society and its Laws, but rather on how people have thought of that relationship. My focus will be on the United States, and on the attitudes of laymen, the consumers of the law.

In taking the layman's point of view, I will use no technical or philosophical definition but rather prefer the common dictionary definition of law: "All the rules of conduct established and enforced by the authority, legislation, or custom of a given community or other group." I will explore a few of the changing ways in which thoughtful laymen in America have come to look on the relation between these rules and all the rest of their social experience. How have literate, self-conscious Americans thought about the relation between their law and their society? What have they wanted to believe? I will be concerned with some examples, in this area, of what William James called the Will to Believe, and it would not be inaccurate to say I am concerned with some "Varieties of Legal Experience."

SOME PECULIAR PROBLEMS OF
MAJORITY-MADE LAW

One of the difficulties of talking about the relation between law and society is that in law, as in all other deep human concerns, the demands we make of our world are contradictory. We wish to believe both that our laws come from a necessity beyond our reach, and that they are our own instruments shaping our community to our chosen ends. We wish to believe that our laws are both changeless and changeable, divine and secular, permanent and temporary, transcendental and pragmatic. These demands are perhaps no more contradictory than those we make of the world when we think of mortality, love, our personal choice of vocation, or our national destiny.

The progress of man, Alfred North Whitehead has shrewdly observed, depends largely on his ability to accept superficial paradoxes, to see that what at first looks like a contradiction need not always remain one. It must have seemed odd to the first man who tried a raft or a bridge that he could cross over a stream of water and not get wet. Now, in modern legal history, the paradox which modern man has learned to live with is that though he can somehow make his own laws, yet they can have an authority above and beyond him.

The discovery, or even the belief, that man could make his own laws, was burdensome. Formerly man could find authority for his laws in the mysterious sanction of ancient practice "to which the mind of man runneth not to the contrary," or in a misty divinity. When, however, men came to see that they, or some majority of them, were the sources of the law, much of the charm melted away. Many men had doubted the wisdom of their kings or their priests. But nearly every man knew in his own heart the vagueness of his own knowledge and the uncertainty of his own wisdom about his society. Scrupulous men were troubled to think that their society was governed by a wisdom no greater than their own.

"Laws that emanate from the people," Orestes A. Brownson wrote in 1873, "or that are binding only by virtue of the assent of the governed, or that emanate from any human source alone, have none of the essential characteristics of law, for they bind no conscience, and restrain, except by force, no will." Brownson had been led to this conclusion by his interpretation of American history and his views of the

American scene. He had taken an active part in the "Hard Cider" presidential campaign of 1840, on the side of the losing Democratic candidate Martin Van Buren, whom he believed to be "the last first-class man that sat, or probably that ever will sit, in the presidential chair of the United States." "What I saw served to dispel my democratic illusions, to break the idol I had worshipped, and shook to its foundation my belief in the divinity of the people, or in their will as the expression of eternal justice." In search of a higher authority, Brownson took refuge in the Roman Catholic Church.

Of course, most Americans have not been so deeply disturbed by this problem. They have preferred to believe that the trouble has not been in the source of the authority, but in how the authority was exercised. That if the people were not yet able to make good laws for themselves, it was not because somebody else should make their laws for them, but because the people were not yet literate enough, or wise enough, or pure enough in their motives.

The rise of self-conscious law-making has remained, however, a parable of the peculiar problems of modern man. Man's growing control over nature has given him an unprecedented power to move about the earth, to reproduce the objects he needs, and to make images of nature. The Industrial Revolution in England and elsewhere in Europe, and the American (or mass-production) system of manufacturing permitted man to surround himself with objects of his own making, to shape his environment to his own needs and desires, and even to his whims. And, incidentally, this allowed him to get in his own way or in the way of his neighbors, as he had never before imagined. In England this worried people like Ruskin and Matthew Arnold; in America it troubled fewer, but there were still some, like Brownson and Thoreau. The sentiment was summed up in Disraeli's aphorism that "Man is not the creature of circumstances. Circumstances are the creatures of men." The new sciences of sociology, psychology, and anthropology further heightened the self-consciousness of man's power to make himself.

Man's power to make his own laws was, despite everything, the most burdensome of his new responsibilities for himself and the universe. His new powers to make things and his powers over nature would have worried him much less if somehow he had felt confident that his laws were rooted outside his society. But in acquiring his mastery over nature he had acquired the guilty secret that his laws might be rooted only in his version of the needs of his time and place.

Now the two contrary beliefs which we still want to hold are (a) that our laws are immanent (or the mere symptom of an indwelling necessity) and (b) that our laws are instrumental (tools we shape to our chosen ends). These two emphases correspond roughly to the two great stages in the development of law which were described by Sir Henry Maine —the movement from customary law or divinely given codes to legislative law. I prefer to call these the successive stages of unselfconscious law-making and self-conscious lawmaking. But the rise of self-conscious law-making does not abolish the need for belief in immanence, it merely transforms that belief. It makes the need for that belief more acute. Now men are burdened not only because they make their particular laws, but because they realize that they have the power to make their very concept of law.

This leads us to the most tantalizing problem—the mystery—of law in modern society. How retain any belief in the immanence of law, in its superiority to our individual, temporary needs, after we have adopted a wholehearted modern belief in its instrumentality? How continue to believe that something about our law is changeless after we have discovered that it may be infinitely plastic? How believe that in some sense the basic laws of society are given us by God, after we have become convinced that we have given them to ourselves?

How persuade ourselves that our laws can be both ancient and up-to-date, when almost nothing else we know has these contrary virtues? Under the older (immanent) view there were no good laws or bad laws, but only laws more or less established, more or less clearly revealed; under the later (instrumental) view there can be good laws, bad laws, better laws, worse laws, laws more effective or less effective. In the United States today we still want to believe that the laws of our community are somehow an inseparable part of our being, of the laws of the universe, of the order of nature, of God's plan for us. Yet we wish also to believe that these have been shaped primarily by our will—the will of the people—and that they are well shaped to the ends which our community has freely chosen.

LEGAL IMMANENCE: TWO EARLIER
AMERICAN EXAMPLES

In modern America, the subtlest problem has been how to retain a balanced sense of legal immanence. Many modern tendencies in social science push us toward extreme dogmas of the instrumental nature of law. Before describing the peculiar problems of finding legal immanence in twentieth-century America, I would like to illustrate what I mean by belief in the immanence of law by two examples. Both are taken from American history before the middle of the nineteenth century: before the flowering of modern social science, and before the rise of pragmatism as an explicit philosophy (or substitute for philosophy).

Personal Perfectionism: The Quakers
of Colonial Pennsylvania

It is hard to find a better example of belief in an indwelling law than among the Quakers of colonial Pennsylvania. For the English Quakers in the seventeenth century the law took its proper shape from the very nature of God, man, and society. This law was supposed to prevail against all the commands of the state. George Fox had exhorted, "My friends . . . going over to plant, and to make outward plantations in America, keep your own plantations in your hearts, with the spirit and power of God, that your own vines and lilies be not hurt." But William Penn, founder of Pennsylvania, was a very sensible man, a man of this world and no mean politician. His Preface to his "Frame of Government for Pennsylvania" (1682) was one of the wisest political manifestoes of the age. In it he warned against excessive faith in any form of government or of laws:

> Any government is free to the people under it (whatever be the frame) where the laws rule, and the people are a party to those laws, and more than this is tyranny, oligarchy, or confusion. But, lastly, when all is said, there is hardly one frame of government in the world so ill designed by its first founders, that, in good hands, would not do well enough. . . . Governments, like clocks, go from the motion men give them; and as governments are made and moved by men, so by them they are ruined too. Wherefore governments rather depend upon men, than men upon governments. Let men be good, and the government cannot be bad; if it be ill, they will cure it. But if men be bad, let the government be never so good, they will endeavour to warp and spoil it to their turn.

Such an emphasis on the indwelling spirit of man as the shaper of society and its laws was the keynote of the Quaker

Colony. For the first half-century of its life, Quaker Pennsylvania flourished, and it remained decisively Quaker. Although sects struggled among themselves, the Quakers managed to rule.

But by the early decades of the eighteenth century, a great struggle had begun. Politically speaking, it was a struggle between the Quakers, settled mostly in Philadelphia and eastern Pennsylvania, and later immigrants who settled to the westward and were beginning to engulf the Quakers even in their Friendly City. It was also, however, a struggle between two concepts of law. On the one side was the Quaker view of an indwelling law, implanted in man and in society by God's beneficent spirit. On the other side was the view of an instrumental law, a man-shaped tool to protect the society against its enemies foreign and domestic.

The weightiest Quakers obstinately insisted on preserving the purity of the law which dwelt within them. They refused to take oaths, because the indwelling law forbade it; they refused to bear arms, or to support the purchase of arms, because their indwelling law was a law of peace; they refused to deal prudently and at arm's-length with the threatening Indians, because their indwelling law of love commanded that the Indians were good, and that they be treated as brothers. The result is now a familiar story. The Quakers were driven from power in the Pennsylvania Assembly in 1756 and became strangers in their own colony. The government of the colony was taken over by non-Quakers, and by the party of the shrewd Benjamin Franklin. From rulers of a society, the Quakers became prophets of a sect. Thereafter they gave most of their energy to reforming their own members, to building miscellaneous humanitarian institutions, and to stirring the larger community toward specific, seemingly utopian reforms. They agitated against slavery and the slave-trade, they worked to humanize prisons and insane-asylums, they built hospitals, they opposed war on principle. Although a long political struggle had been needed to displace them from power, their fate had actually been sealed a century before when a Quaker Yearly Meeting had declared: "The setting up and putting down Kings and Governments is God's peculiar prerogative, for causes best known to himself."

The Pennsylvania Quaker experience in the eighteenth century dramatized on the American colonial stage both the strengths and the weaknesses of one extreme form of belief in the immanence of law. Rigid and changeless, it was a law of self-righteousness—of the righteousness of the self. But it was a law careless of its effects, more concerned for self than for community, blind to the needs of suffering women and children in the Indian-harried backwoods. It was a law of intransigent individuals. Inevitably Quaker law became a sectarian credo rather than the foundation of a large society.

Certain features of the Quaker law must be noted. The Quakers were an untheoretical, untheological, unlegislative people. Their law was untechnical. Their law consisted in a few general tenets: love, peace, no swearing, all men are good. Paradoxically, its very unsystematic, unwritten, untechnical character made the Quakers the more fearful of bending any provisions of their law to the needs of community.

These rigid, unrealistic qualities of Quaker law were not the necessary consequences of a belief in God, or in a divine foundation for society. Less than three hundred miles away were the New England Puritans. The laws of Puritanism were highly elaborated, very much written, and not lacking in technicality. In the long run the written, technical, elaborated laws of the Bibliolatrous New England Puritans— God-based though they were—proved far more flexible than the unwritten, inarticulate, untechnical benevolent spirit which governed the Pennsylvania Quakers.

Social Narcissism: The Ante-Bellum South

Another, and in many ways contrasting, form of belief in immanent law developed in the Southern United States in the half-century before the Civil War. It shared many of the formal features of the colonial Pennsylvanian law of the Quakers: it, too, was unwritten, inarticulate, untechnical, and unbending. But it differed in its content, its source, and its sanction.

The rise in the South of belief in immanent law must be explained by two dominant facts of Southern life in this period. The first was the institution of slavery; the second was the defensive spirit, the feeling that the whole Southern society was under attack from the outside.

The great planters ran their affairs by informal understandings, gentlemen's agreements, and pledges of honor. Surprisingly little legal paper was used in the conduct of the Southern plantation and Southern commerce in the early years of the nineteenth century. This is, of course, one of the reasons why it is hard to learn as much as we would like about the daily life of the time. The tendency to rely on unwritten rules was accentuated by the existence of slavery and by the very character of that institution. Slavery was a labor-system in which the rules were local custom or the arbitrary decision of the master. Since the common law of England did not recognize the status of slavery, there was no developed body of law concerning slavery, the rights of the slave, or the duties of the master in the English slaveholding colonies. By contrast, as has often been noted, Latin America and the Caribbean areas governed by the Roman law transmitted through Spain or Portugal, had a highly developed law of slavery with traditions and practices reaching back to ancient times.

An ironic result of the fact that English law favored liberty and refused to recognize slavery was thus that the Negro slave in the English colonies was a mere chattel, with virtually no recognizable legal personality, and few if any rights against his master. He was in many ways worse off than were slaves in a society that had inherited a long tradition of legalized slavery. The legal situation of the slave in the Southern United States was further worsened by the failure of Protestantism to take the strong religious-equalitarian stand of Catholicism, and by the indelible identification of race with the status of slavery. In Roman law, slavery was, of course, a legal status independent of race; and as the slave laws of Cuba, for example, developed, they recognized gradations of servitude and racial gradations (mulatto, quadroon, octoroon, etc.). But in the North American English colonies and in the States derived from them slavery was an all-or-nothing proposition.

Another striking fact about the institution of slavery in the Ante-Bellum South is not merely the meagre or nonexistent rights of the Negro slave, but the meagre amount of legal literature concerning the laws of slavery. Slave codes were sparse and did not purport to cover all possible situations. Even treatises on slavery were few and far between. The best legal treatises of the age on American Negro slavery (with the conspicious exception only of Cobb's *Law of Negro Slavery*, 1858) did not come from the South at all, but were written in New York or Philadelphia.

When the Southerner confronted this fact of the sparseness of the formal legal rights of the Negro and the meagreness of written law, he began to discover, by the 1840's and 1850's, that these symbolized the virtues of the South's peculiar institution. Not only extremist defenders of slavery, like George Fitzhugh, but other loyal Southerners as well, argued that this distinction between the legalistic, pettifogging, literal-minded, mean-spirited North—with its eye always on written records and the cash-box—and on the other hand, the generous, chivalrous, kind-hearted, honorgoverned South, expressed the whole difference between their institutions.

"Human Law," Fitzhugh explained in *Cannibals All! or, Slaves without Masters* (1857), "cannot beget benevolence, affection, maternal and paternal love; nor can it supply their places; but it may, by breaking up the ordinary relations of human beings, stop and disturb the current of these finer feelings of our nature. It may abolish slavery; but it can never create between the capitalist and the laborer, between employer and employed, the kind and affectionate relations that usually exist between master and slave." The essence of slavery, Southern defenders argued, was that it did not depend on explicit, instrumental rules; and this was precisely its virtue. For, under slavery, they said, the laws of employment became one with the natural currents of social sentiment on both sides: kindness and generosity on the side of the employer, loyalty and industry on the side of the employed. "Experience and observation fully satisfy me," remarked Judge O'Neall of South Carolina in 1853, "that the first law of slavery is that of kindness from the master to the slave . . . slavery becomes a family relation, next in its attachments to that of parent and child."

To understand the Southern law of slavery, then, you could not look at the lawbooks, but instead had to observe the actual ways of the community. The defense of slavery became more and more a defense of the unwritten law, the immanent law, the ways which dwelt in the ongoing Southern society, or as it was sometimes said, in the Southern Way of Life.

The South then came to idealize the unwritten law, which was said to be the only proper law for a Christian society, an ennobling influence on all who allowed themselves to be ruled by it. Just as slavery made it possible for the relations between superior and inferior to be governed in this fashion, so, too, a code of "honor" made it possible for relations among equals to be similarly governed. And the gentlemen of the Southern ruling class spurned the letter of the law which, in the Southern States, as elsewhere, forbade the duel and punished it as homicide. They actually made resort to the duel (the "Code of Honor") a symbol of their respect for the immanent as against the instrumental law of the community. In the South, in the half-century before the Civil War, there was hardly a leader in public life who had not fought a duel. Much as a war-record nowadays attests a man's high devotion to his community, and is supposed to help qualify him for public office, so in those days, having fought an "affair of honor" proved a gentleman to be a "man of honor," for it showed that he held the immanent law of the society above its petty explicit rules.

The Southern defense of its immanent law, of the actual rules by which the South lived, against the attacks by literal-minded, casual travelers and bookish Northerners who judged all societies by their written rules—this itself became a defense of the Southern Way of Life. Southerners were increasingly wholistic and mystical in their praise of their institutions. Southern Ways, they declared, fitted together so neatly and so subtly, that one dared not jar them by tinkering with the explicit rules.

Southerners became social narcissists. What were the proper virtues of any society, what were the laws by which any society should be ruled? Look at the South and you would see. Not at the rules in books, or the statutes passed by legislatures, or the decisions of judges (there were precious few of these anyway), but at the society itself, at how it actually worked. The proper laws of the South, it was said again and again, dwelt in the actual ways of the South. For the laws of its society the South came more and more to look in the mirror.

The consequences of this increasingly intransigent, increasingly narrow, increasingly inward and tautologous way of looking at law were, of course, to be far-reaching. They were tragic for the nation, and still remain tragic for the South. But we need not follow them out in detail to see that the South had developed an extreme and uncompromising belief in the immanence of law. The Southerners, we might say, had developed an odd kind of social Quakerism. The Quakers were a "peculiar people" (so they called themselves); the Southerners lived by their "peculiar institution." The Quakers lived by a law which dwelt in each individual, and against which there could be no proper appeal to statute books, legislatures or law-courts. The Southerners too lived by a law which dwelt in their society, and against which they believed there could be no appeal. Both societies had chosen to live by an immanent law: unwritten, inarticulate, untechnical, and unbending.

LEGAL IMMANENCE: THE FEDERAL
CONSTITUTION AND THE FOUR FREEDOMS

Belief in the immanence of law runs deep in our American tradition. In the story of the development of our institutions what distinguishes both the Quakers of colonial Pennsylvania and the Ante-Bellum Southerners is not their belief in some form of legal immanence, but the extreme and intransigent intensity of their belief.

A striking feature of our history is how few examples we offer of individuals or communities embracing a radically instrumental theory of law. Jeremy Bentham, therefore, is one of the most un-American of English thinkers. Few nations have legislated more than the United States, or put more faith in legislation; few have put less faith in any explicit theory of legislation. Traditional legal learning has sometimes been overvalued here because of its scarcity, but it has generally commanded the same naïve respect accorded to all ancient lineages in raw countries.

In this New World, where men have so often boasted of their opportunity to make a New Beginning, movements to codify or new-fashion laws have made surprisingly little headway. In the early nineteenth century, which was an age of codes and radical legislation in Western Europe, we were making constitutions and elaborating an American common law. Even in England, much of the legal history of the nineteenth century can be written around movements self-consciously to change society by using law as a tool; in the twentieth century there have been triumphs of intricate and subtle codification, like the Real Property Act of 1928. But in the United States, while we have codified some of our procedure and made some headway toward Uniform State Laws, even in this century our distinctive contributions have been our modest efforts to draw the private law together and to make it accessible rather than boldly to reshape it to serve new social needs. Perhaps our most distinctive contributions have been our extra-legal devices for indexing, key-numbering, and collecting cases. Our great twentieth-century effort to reformulate the law has produced informal "Restatements" rather than revisions or codifications.

We have been a nation, then, of many laws, but of few

law-reforms. The circumstances of our American Revolution had encouraged belief that the laws of our nation were not malleable instruments to attain specific social purposes, but were part of our very being. We inherited a legal system which was brought here in the very minds of the settlers. We had no self-conscious "reception" of the common law comparable to that which agitated the European Continent. Our legal theory could thus remain impressively inarticulate, while Continental legal thinkers asked again and again how laws could be used to serve social ends. What, they asked, was the proper relation between law and society? What were the healthiest roots of laws?

Savigny and Jhering remained even more exotic than Bentham; to this day they are hardly known among American lawyers. Here there was no widespread open battle between legal systems. Our battle was only among jurisdictions. Our common law had come with us. Since no conscious act of adoption or acceptance was ever needed, we continued to see a certain inevitability about our whole system of law. The common law and its tradition of constitutionalism seemed part of the very fibre of our social being. We embraced the Blackstonian view (which in England even by the time of our Revolution was coming to seem obsolete) that the common law was a providential embodiment of Reason and Nature. We inherited a great legal literature, which summed up the general rules without our ever having been required to make those rules, or even to make the effort of "discovering" them.

One symptom of the relatively minor role we have given legislation as an instrument for social change is the extraordinary importance we have given to constitutions. What Willard Hurst calls our tradition of "constitution worship" has embodied the still deeper tradition that our laws must somehow be the expressers rather than the shapers of our society.

American tradition has, of course, given a mystic role to the framers of the Federal Constitution. They have been adored for what we suppose to have been a declaratory rather than a creative act. Again and again we have held that they surely revealed the innermost spirit of the new American nation, and embodied it in words.

"The system is no invention of man," a nineteenth-century writer observed, "is no creation of the [Constitutional] convention, but is given us by Providence in the living constitution of the American people. The merit of the statesmen of 1787 is that they did not destroy or deface the work of Providence, but accepted it and organized the government in harmony with the real order, the real elements given them. They suffered themselves in all their positive substantial work to be governed by reality, not by theories and speculations."

When Justice Samuel F. Miller of the Supreme Court spoke in 1887 at the centennial celebration of the framing of the Federal Constitution he recalled George Bancroft's description of the last hours of the Convention: "The members were awestruck at the results of their councils, the Constitution was a nobler work than anyone of them had believed possible to achieve." Justice Miller himself expressed his satisfaction that the Constitution had originally been intended to establish a truly national government. This tradition, of course, continues. W. W. Crosskey's weighty *Politics and the Constitution* (1953) again aimed to prove that the providential foresight of the Framers envisioned precisely the kind of national government which was most convenient to handle the problems of the national economy under Franklin Delano Roosevelt.

For us, the idea of a constitution—a fundamental law which in some strange way is less changeable than the ordinary instruments of legislation—has had a peculiar therapeutic attraction. Since 1776, there have been over two hundred state conventions to adopt or revise constitutions. Yet we have seldom amended our Federal Constitution and it remains the oldest working written constitution in the Western World. We retain an incurable belief that constitutions are born but not made, and this despite the carelessness, prolixity, crudity, and proven ineptitude of many of our State constitutions.

The two great armed conflicts on our soil, the American Revolution and the Civil War, were both victories for legal orthodoxy, for traditional legal doctrines—at least according to the victors. We have a remarkable continuity in our political and legal history. Any decisive innovations in our institutions (for example, those induced by the Depression of 1929–) have sooner or later been hallowed by the Supreme Court. The Court certifies that the laws required by newly emerging problems somehow were implied and authorized in the very charter of our national existence. The continuous power and dignity of the Supreme Court make the Court a distinctive American embodiment of belief in the immanence of our laws. Despite everything, we insist on believing that what the Court does is not to make the law but to declare it: not *jus dare* but *jus dicere*.

Never yet have we experienced a forcible deflection of our national institutions by arms, by coup d'état, or the seizure of power by one party or one class. Thus we have never really been jolted into seeing laws as the mere instruments of power. But in this as in so many other ways, the South has been an exception.

Since the early years of the twentieth century events on the international scene have pushed us as a nation toward an increasing belief in legal immanence. More and more we have come to believe that a nation's laws are not mere instruments toward ends, but are themselves essential to the character of the society, inseparable from the society, an indwelling expression of a nation's purposes.

This movement toward a wider belief in the oneness of a society's laws with its ends is illustrated by the contrast between our stated national objectives in World War I and in World War II. There is a striking contrast between the kind of objectives stated by President Woodrow Wilson in his "Fourteen Points" (Annual Address to Congress, January 8, 1918) and those stated by President Franklin Delano Roosevelt in his "Four Freedoms" (Annual Address to Congress, January 6, 1941). President Wilson itemized a number of objectives on the international scene. These were quite specific political and economic readjustments, for example: reduction of armaments, the impartial settlement of colonial claims, the evacuation of Russia, the restoration of Belgium, the freeing of invaded portions of France, the adjustment of the frontiers of Italy, the autonomy of the peoples of Austria-Hungary, etc. etc. Such objectives required laws for their accomplishment, but the objectives were plainly separate from the laws.

President Roosevelt's "Four Freedoms" Speech, on the other hand, described perils to "the democratic way of life" which was "assailed in every part of the world." His "Four essential human freedoms"—freedom of speech and expression; freedom of every person to worship God in his own way; freedom from want; and freedom from fear—were called way-of-life objectives. They were not political aims to be attained by legal tools. Rather the aims themselves were as much legal as political. A nation's laws now were the touchstone. Laws were assumed to be not a mere instrument but the primary expression of its way of life. From the

American point of view the conflict was between law-loving, law-fearing societies, and others.

In the three decades after our entry into World War I, leading Americans had ceased to believe that on the international scene the United States was concerned merely with the preservation of a political system. What had to be defended, we heard again and again, was a "Way of Life." The terrors of totalitarian democracies—of dictatorships which actually could claim to express the will of the majority of their people—revealed that the mere fact that a government represented a current majority was no guarantee of decency or of respect for human rights. Only slowly did Americans abandon the political fallacy. They hung on to their belief, which many have not yet abandoned, that if a government outraged decency then, *ex hypothesi,* it could not express the will of the majority of its people. But it has lately dawned on more and more of us that political democracy is only one element and not enough in itself to insure decent institutions. Way of life means much more. It includes a society's laws, and its attitude toward its laws. The traditional American distrust of legal instrumentalism has been expressed anew in a popular antipathy to "isms": fear of any concept of society that would abstract and dogmatize national objectives, and then use its laws as mere tools to those ends.

TEMPTATIONS TO A MIRROR-VIEW

As I remarked at the outset, the balance between legal immanence and legal instrumentalism is the mysterious balance of law in society. It is one of the subtlest problems of every age. We face it once again in our time—in the pressures all around us to believe that force successfully exerted by small groups within our society must be accepted as law.

We have seen that the kind of immanence which people find in the law, and which can satisfy their belief that the law is not arbitrary or purely instrumental, varies a great deal. It is far too narrow to identify this belief exclusively with natural law or with a belief in God. In the Soviet Union, and perhaps in other communist countries, it seems possible for people to have this satisfaction of a belief in legal immanence by seeing their laws as a manifestation of rules indwelling in history, as expounded in the Gospel according to Marx, Lenin, Stalin, and their followers. In Nazi Germany people secured it by belief in a racial destiny, an indwelling "law of the folk"—expounded in the Gospel according to Hitler, Rosenberg, and Goebbels. We are too ready from our provincial point of view to view totalitarianism as a barefaced unhallowed instrumentalism, in which rulers use the law for their own ends. But this is not how such systems look to their supporters, from the inside. These peoples have not given up the need to find some immanence —some transcendental-indwelling validity in their laws. Rather they find forms of immanence unfamiliar to us. We have yet to see a government that has ruled a society effectively without providing its people with some persuasive way of believing that their laws come from some higher, deeper, indwelling source.

In the United States the kind of belief in immanence which has been growing in the last half-century, bears, superficially at least, some discomfiting similarities to that which I have described in the Southern States before the Civil War. Although the content is very different, the formal character of the beliefs and some of the surrounding circumstances are quite comparable. Our belief in legal immanence has arisen out of a dominant—one might almost say a fetishistic—belief in the peculiar virtue and perfection of political democracy as we know it, and as it is practiced in the United States. And *our* belief, too, has been a kind of response to outside attack. In order to strengthen ourselves against the threat of communist conspiracy and totalitarian subversion we take a wholistic view. While Southerners came to see the institution of slavery as the lifeblood of all social good, nourishing the peculiar virtues of political, social, economic, and cultural life in the South, so we see our institution of political democracy informing our political, social, economic, and cultural life. Just as the Southerners saw a peril, not only to their political system and their economy, but to their whole Way of Life, so with us. With the increase of Northern threats the intransigence of Southerners' belief in themselves and their peculiar institution hardened. Their belief in immanence was expressed in their faith in a law which was unwritten, untechnical, and unbending. And so is ours.

I have characterized the Ante-Bellum Southern belief in immanence as a tendency toward "Social Narcissism." The society came to worship itself. Reform movements virtually disappeared. Southern thinkers came to confuse sociology with social morality. They looked into the mirror to see what they should be. Certain tendencies in American life today suggest that we too are in danger of finding our immanence in the mirror. We are tempted to allow brute power, wherever displayed or threatened, to become the measure of law.

In the last half-century, the predominant fact of intellectual history shaping our thinking about law and society has been the rise of the social sciences, and the idea of social science. Only a few decades ago courses in sociology in better colleges were still entitled "The Prevention of Poverty." They were primarily concerned with such topics as crime, delinquency, and "the social evil." But nowadays sociology is concerned with "techniques of social control," the structure of society, the functions of cities, and the roles of social classes and races. The study of government has become "political science"; political economy has become the science of economics. Even history has become more and more social-scientific. *An American Dilemma: the Negro Problem and Modern Democracy,* a collaborative work in social sciences by Gunnar Myrdal and many others, was published in 1944. The unanimous Supreme Court decision declaring racial segregation in the public schools unconstitutional came exactly ten years later, in 1954. The "future" which Justice Holmes in his "Path of the Law" (1897) predicted would belong to "the man of statistics and the master of economics"—that future has now arrived.

The conviction grows—and is expressed in the curricula of our best law schools—that the lawyer must not only know law. He must know the facts of life, the facts of our society, the laws of social behavior inherent in society itself. Only recently have we begun to act on the truism that one cannot know a society's laws without knowing the society. There are obviously many advantages, for the lawyer, and for the society.

But with this belief comes the tendency to find the immanence of the law in the supposedly inevitable tendencies of the society itself. It has often been remarked that Justice Holmes' description of the object of legal study as "prediction, the prediction of the incidence of the public force through the instrumentality of the courts," while helpful to the practicing lawyer, is not very useful to the legislator, the citizen, or the social scientist trying to decide how legal development should be directed. The great danger of the social-science emphasis in the training of lawyers, the great danger of finding the immanence of our law in the very processes of our society, is that we should make law into tautology. The predictive theory of law could lead us to make all our society's laws nothing but self-fulfilling prophecies. Obviously, our laws cannot ignore the facts of our social life, but they must do more than merely reflect them. Intelligent citizens cannot be guided by what their opinion polls tell them is their opinion.

We suffer ever-stronger temptations to social narcissism. In a beleaguered world we are ever more tempted to be satisfied that our laws should reflect a society which we define as *ex hypothesi* good. But to do so is to deprive our laws of the normative role which, in the common law tradition, has made them a bulwark for each generation against the specious urgencies of its own age.

One of the most difficult problems in our society today is to get a message in from the outside. We believe in our power to make ourselves. The more we see our laws as a reflection of norms indwelling in current social practice, pressures, and disorders, the more we deprive ourselves of an opportunity to make law a means of communication between the past and the present. For this purpose the preservation of a tradition of professionalism, of technicality, is essential. Here we must more than ever rely on what Coke —against the arbitrary James I, the amateur lawyer who said he knew all he needed to know of the law—said was not natural reason but "the artificial reason and judgment of the law, which law is an art which requires long study and experience, before that a man can attain to the cognizance of it."

LAW AS PROPAGANDA

The temptations to tautology, to a mirror-view of the law, to a doctrine of immanence which finds the purposes and forms of the law in the most pressing needs of our own day, are increased by the pressures we feel from abroad. Our temptation is to make the social sciences a body of knowledge for fashioning the law into a better mirror of what our society already is. But the challenge of totalitarianism and the desire to confront the world with our "Way of Life" press us to make our law an instrument of propaganda.

The use of international trials, under cover of law, as an instrument of political persuasion and diplomacy is an example. Such trials are a peculiar feature of our age. After World War II, the "War Crimes Trials"—designed, among other things, to dramatize our Way of Life and contrast it with totalitarian ways—made law into propaganda.

When future generations read the proceedings of the Nuremberg Trials, where the criminals were prosecuted by a Justice of the United States Supreme Court who had stepped down from his bench specifically for this purpose and where the accused were adjudged by representatives of the victorious powers, it is doubtful if they will see it as a triumph of law. Although the background in each case was of course very different, and the truth of the charges varied vastly, it is more likely that the War Crimes Trials of 1946 will be classed with the Reichstag Fire Trial (1933–34), the so-called Trial of the Trotskyite-Zinovievite Terrorist Centre (1936), the Moscow Trials of the "Anti-Soviet 'Bloc of Rights and Trotskyites' " (1938), the Japanese War Crimes Trials (1946–48) and the Eichmann Trial (1961) as examples of use of the forms of legality for political and propaganda purposes. The readiness of a country like Israel to use kidnapping to bring international criminals before the bar of "legality" illustrates where the modern propagandistic use of law can lead us. We move toward an unalloyed legal instrumentalism, in the name of a higher law.

Our position before the world makes it increasingly difficult for us to satisfy our need for an immanent law without giving in to the temptations to make our law unwritten, untechnical, and unbending. How can we satisfy our need to find immanence in our law without making it a mere name for lawlessness? Our lawyers can help by perpetuating their professional esprit and their pride of specialized knowledge. But here is also a problem for laymen. Every society is apt to think too well of itself, to exaggerate its urgencies, against the claims which the past has on it, or the debt it owes to the future. How can our society find and preserve that mysterious balance between the implicit and the explicit, the immanent and the instrumental, which our legal tradition requires of us? Only such a balance can preserve our tradition of a society ruled by law.

V

DISSENT,

 DISSENSION,

AND THE NEWS

Dissent is the great problem of America today. It overshadows all others. It is a symptom, an expression, a consequence, and a cause of all others.

I say dissent and not disagreement. And it is the distinction between dissent and disagreement which I really want to make. Disagreement produces debate but dissent produces dissension. Dissent (which comes from the Latin, *dis* and *sentire*) means originally to feel apart from others.

People who disagree have an argument, but people who dissent have a quarrel. People may disagree and both may count themselves in the majority. But a person who dissents is by definition in a minority. A liberal society thrives on disagreement but is killed by dissension. Disagreement is the life blood of democracy, dissension is its cancer.

A debate is an orderly exploration of a common problem that presupposes that the debaters are worried by the same question. It brings to life new facts and new arguments which make possible a better solution. But dissension means discord. As the dictionary tells us, dissension is marked by a break in friendly relations. It is an expression not of a common concern but of hostile feelings. And this distinction is crucial.

THE LAW OF THE
CONSPICUOUSNESS OF DISSENT

Disagreement is specific and programmatic, dissent is formless and unfocused. Disagreement is concerned with policy, dissenters are concerned with identity, which usually means themselves. Disagreers ask, what about the war in Vietnam? Dissenters ask, what about me? Disagreers seek solutions to common problems, dissenters seek power for themselves.

The spirit of dissent stalks our land. It seeks the dignity and privilege of disagreement, but it is entitled to neither. All over the country on more and more subjects we hear more and more people quarreling and fewer and fewer people debating. How has this happened? What can and what should we do about it?

This is my question. In the first place I would like to remind you of one feature of the situation which suggests that it may not be as desperate as it seems. This is what I would call the Law of the Conspicuousness of Dissent. This Law is another way of saying that there never is quite as much dissent as there seems.

I will start from an oddity of the historical record.

When we try to learn, for example, about the history of religion in the United States we find that what is generally called by that name is a history of religious controversies. It is very easy to learn about the Halfway Covenant problem, the Great Awakening, the Unitarian debates, the "Americanist" struggle within the Catholic Church, and so on. But if we want to learn about the current of daily belief of Americans in the past it is very difficult.

And this is a parable of the problem of all history. If we want to learn about the history of divorce there are many excellent histories of divorce, but if we want to learn about the history of marriage or the family we find that for the United States at least, there are few books to help us.

Similarly if we want to learn about eating and drinking habits there are some excellent histories of vegetarianism and food fads, some first-rate histories of prohibition but almost no good histories of eating and drinking.

Why is this the case?

Controversies, quarrels, disagreements leave a historical debris of printed matter—not to mention broken heads and broken reputations. Carry Nation smashing up a bar makes much more interesting reading and is more likely to enter the record than the peaceable activity of the bartender mixing drinks. But this may lead us to a perverse emphasis. How have people lived and thought and felt and eaten and drunk and married in the past? Our interest tends to be focused on the cataracts, the eddies, the waterfalls, and the whirlpools. But what of the main stream?

This is a natural bias of the record, and it equally affects the reporting of news. A sermon is generally less newsworthy than a debate and a debate still less newsworthy than a riot. This is all obvious, but it has serious consequences for the condition of our country today. For the natural bias of the record leads us to emphasize—and inevitably then to overemphasize—the extent of dissent.

The conspicuousness of dissent comes also from the mere rise and multiplication of media. The elaboration of our newspaper and magazine press, of radio and television, together with the American standard of living leads us also to exaggerate the importance of dissent in our society. Since

dissent is more dramatic and more newsworthy than agreement, media inevitably multiply and emphasize dissent. It is
an easier job to make a news story of men who are fighting
one another than it is to describe their peaceful living together.

All this has been reenforced by certain obvious developments in the history of the newspaper and other media
within the last half-century and especially by the increasingly frequent and repetitious news reporting. The movement from the weekly newspaper to the daily newspaper to
several editions a day, the rise of radio-reporting of news
every hour on the hour with news breaks in between, all
require that there be changes to report. There are increasingly voluminous spaces both of time and of print which
have to be filled.

And all these reports become more and more inescapable
from the attention of the average citizen. In the bar, on the
beach, in the automobile, the transistor radio reminds us of
the headaches of our society. Moreover, the increasing viv-
idness of reports also tempts us to depict objects and people
in motion, changing, disputing. The opportunity to show
people in motion and to show them vividly had its beginning, of course, in the rise of photography, in Mathew
Brady's pioneer work in the Civil War, and then more recently with the growth of the motion picture and television.
We are tempted to go in search of a dramatic shot of a po-
liceman striking a rioter or vice versa. And on the scene we
now have tape recorders in which people can express their
complaints about anything.

The rise of opinion has given us a new category for publi-
cized dissent. The growth of opinion polling has led to the
very concept of "opinion" as something people can learn
about. There was a time when information about the world
was divided into the category of fact or the category of

ideas. But more recently, especially with the growth of market research in this century, people must have opinions. They are led to believe by the publication of opinion polls that their opinion—whether on miniskirts or marijuana or foreign policy—is something that separates them from others. If they have no opinion, even that now puts them in a distinct category.

Then there is the rise of what I call secondary news. News about the news. With an increasingly sophisticated readership and more and more media we have such questions as whether a news conference will be canceled. Will someone refuse to make a statement? Was the fact that the then Jacqueline Kennedy denied there was a supposed engagement between her and Lord Harlech itself a kind of admission? What is really news?

The very character of American history has accentuated our tendency to dissent. For we are an immigrant society, made up of many different groups who came here feeling separate from one another, and who often were separated not so much by doctrine or belief as by the minutiae of daily life. By language, religious practices, cuisine, and even manners. Until the 1930's and 40's, the predominant aim of those in this country who were most concerned with the problem of immigration was to restrict immigration or to assimilate those immigrants who were admitted. "Americanize the Immigrant"—this was their motto.

But in the last few decades we have had a movement from "assimilation" to "integration." And this is an important distinction. Louis Adamic's *A Nation of Nations* (1945) gave classic statement to a position that became more and more popular. It was no longer the right of the immigrant to be Americanized, to be assimilated. It was now the right of the immigrant to remain different, not to be "assimilated" but to be "integrated."

The ideal ceased to be that of fitting into the total society and instead became the right to retain your differences. Symptoms of this were such phenomena in politics as the rise of the balanced ticket, a ticket which consists of outspoken and obvious representatives of different minorities. It brought with it the assumption that the only 100 per cent American is the person who is only partly American. It led General Eisenhower to make something of his German name and his German background which had not occurred to very many of us before. It encouraged John F. Kennedy to exploit his Irish background, the notion being that one was more fully American by being partly something else.

THE RISE OF MINORITY VETO

This sense of the separateness and the power of minorities developed alongside two great movements. One, in the social sciences: the growth of a new literature which came to show minorities who they were, where they were, and what their power might be.

Gunnar Myrdal's collaborative book *An American Dilemma,* which was cited in the Supreme Court Integration decision of 1954, was a prominent illustration of this emphasis in the social sciences. The rising science of opinion polling also had the same effect. People in small groups were reminded that they had a power and a locale which they had not so precisely known before. Black Power leaders have referred to this on several occasions—that they may represent a group which is not very numerous but at least they know where they are: in crucial places where they can exercise power.

Alongside this change in our thinking and this extension of our knowledge came a change in technology which I would call the rise of "Flow Technology." Minimum speed forty miles an hour. This means that while formerly, in order to do damage to other people, it was necessary for you to set things in motion—to throw a rock or wield a club —now when the economy and the technology are in motion, if you want to cause damage you need only stop and the other people do the damage. This new opportunity was illustrated in the electrical blackout of November 9, 1965, in New York and is dramatized in stall-ins and sit-ins. When students seize the administration building at a university, all they have to do is to hold that one building. All the salary checks flow through the IBM machines in that building and students in that one place are able to throw a monkey-wrench into the machinery.

This has the effect, too, of developing what I would call a minority-veto psychology. Small groups have more power than ever before. In *small* numbers there is strength. And this, in turn, results in the quest for minority identity. Whereas formerly people used to change their names to sound more American or more WASP-y to try to fit into the background, now the contrary seems to be occurring.

We find symptoms of this desperate quest for minority identity all about us in the intellectual world. Perhaps that is a misnomer—I should say rather in the world of those who consider themselves or call themselves intellectuals. I find in the world of self-styled intellectuals in this country today a growing belief in the intrinsic virtue of dissent. It is worth noting that some of the greatest American champions of the right to disagree and to express disagreement—Thomas Jefferson, Oliver Wendell Holmes, Jr., William James, John Dewey, and others—were also great believers in the duty of the community to be peacefully governed by the will of the majority. But more recently dissent itself has been made into a virtue. Dissent for dissent's sake. We have a whole group of journals and book reviews these days dedicated not to this or that particular program or social reform nor this or that social philosophy but simply to dissent.

Professional dissenters do not and cannot seek to assimilate their program or ideals into American culture. Their main object is to preserve their separate identity as a dissenting minority. They are not interested in the freedom of anybody else. The motto of this group might be an emendation of the old maxim of Voltaire which we have all heard. But nowadays people would say, "I do not agree with a word you say. And I will defend to the death *my* right to say so."

Once upon a time our intellectuals competed for their claim to be spokesmen of the community. Now the time has almost arrived when the easiest way to insult an intellectual is to tell him that you or most other people agree with him. The way to menace him is to put him in the majority, for the majority must run things and must have a program, but dissent needs no program.

THE NEW CONFORMITY OF DISSENT

Dissent, then, has tended to become the conformity of our most educated classes. In those circles to say that the prevailing ways of the community are not "evil" requires more courage than to run with the dissenting pack.

The conformity of nonconformity, the conformity of dissent, produces little that is fruitful in its conclusions and very little effective discussion or internal debate. For the simple reason that it does not involve anybody in attacking or defending any program. Programs, after all, are the signs —and the sins—of "The Establishment."

The situation that I have described leads to certain temptations which afflict the historian as well as the newsman, and among these temptations I would like to include the tendency to stimulate and accentuate dissent rather than disagreement. To push disagreement toward dissent so that we can have a more dramatic or reportable event. To push the statement of a program toward the expression of a feeling of separateness or isolation.

There is an increasing tendency also to confuse disagreement with dissent. For example, the homosexuals in our society, who are a group who feel separate (and are from one point of view a classic example of what we mean by the dissenter), now articulate their views in declarations and statements. They become disagreers, they form Mattachine Societies, they issue programs and declarations. This, I would say, is good.

But on the other hand we find disagreers who are increasingly tempted to use the techniques of dissent. Students who disagree about the war in Vietnam, or Negroes who disagree about urban policies, use the techniques of dissent, of affirming their secession from society, and this is bad.

The expressions of disagreement may lead to better policy but dissent cannot.

The affirmations of differentness and feeling apart cannot hold a society together. In fact these tend to destroy the institutions which make fertile disagreement possible, and fertile institutions decent. A sniper's bullet is an eloquent expression of dissent, of feeling apart. It does not express disagreement. It is formless, inarticulate, unproductive. A society of disagreers is a free and fertile and productive society. A society of dissenters is a chaos leading only to dissension.

Now we are led to a paradox. A paradox which must be resolved. For a free and literate society with a high standard of living and increasingly varied media reaching more and more people more and more of the time finds it always easier to dramatize its dissent rather than its disagreements. And we find it harder and harder to discover, much less to dramatize, our agreement on anything.

We end then with some questions which challenge the men and women who shape and write and produce our newspapers and our programs on radio and television.

First, is it possible to produce interesting newspapers and attractive radio and television programs that will sell but which do not dramatize or capitalize on or catalyze dissent and dissension, the feeling of apartness in the community? Is it possible to produce interesting newspapers and radio and television programs that will sell but which do not yield to the temptation to create and nourish new dissent by stirring people to feel apart in new ways?

Second, is it possible at the same time to find new ways of interesting people in disagreement, in specific items and problems and programs and specific evils?

Finally, is it possible for our media—without becoming pollyannas or chauvinists or super-patriots or Good Humor salesmen—to find new ways of expressing and affirming, dramatizing and illuminating, what people agree upon?

The future of American society may depend on whether and how these questions are answered.

VI

☆

THE END

OF OUR

TWO-PARTY

WORLD

☆

Seldom before in American History has so much "political" activity taken place outside of our political institutions. This is the age of the street demonstration, the sit-in, the teach-in, the shut-down. It is the age of political expression and political frustration. Some say our young people have become too political; others, that they are not political enough. We are confused not only about what our politics ought to be but even about what activity really is, or is not, political. Where does "politics" end, and where does agitation, insurrection, or chaos begin?

Of course, many forces have helped to produce the current confusion. But among the most important is the revolution in our political consciousness. New ways of thinking have put our political world beyond the wildest imaginings of our grandfathers. Yet, while our ways of thinking and feeling and learning about politics have been transformed, our political system has remained virtually unchanged.

The widely heralded changes in our election system have

not been as revolutionary as they seem. They have been only the latest steps along the familiar road of American political history. "Legislators represent people," Chief Justice Warren declared in 1964, "not trees or acres. Legislators are elected by voters, not farms or cities or economic interests." When the Supreme Court recently insisted that congressional districts be reapportioned on this principle, it was taking one late stride toward majority rule.

Much of the history of our political system since the founding of the nation has been the fulfillment of the principle of majority rule—a democracy of numbers—and its victory over competing principles. The Constitutional Convention of 1787 almost broke up because the small states feared that a democracy of regions—the principle of "One state, one vote," under the old Articles of Confederation—would be entirely displaced by a democracy of numbers in which representation would precisely correspond to population. Before the Civil War, John C. Calhoun and other Southern statesmen argued that the Founding Fathers had never intended to set up a democracy of numbers, but instead had aimed that legislators actually should represent "acres" or "economic interests." Fearing the numerical majority, they said that no action of the national government could be law unless every single economic interest agreed. The Civil War was the costly, but decisive, victory for the democracy of numbers.

Since then, we have aimed to make our government more and more a system of majority rule. We have tried to make the electorate an ever-larger proportion of the whole population and to give it more powers. By the time of the Civil War, property qualifications were no longer of much consequence, and the electorate included nearly all adult male white citizens. Six of our constitutional amendments—a greater number than has been devoted to any other single subject since the Bill of Rights, and about half of all those adopted since the Civil War—have concerned the right to vote. Each of these amendments has aimed to make the electorate more numerous.

The 14th and 15th amendments included Negroes; the 17th amendment took the election of senators from the state legislators and gave it to each state's whole electorate; the 19th amendment brought in women; the 23rd amendment gave the presidential franchise to residents of the District of Columbia, and the 24th amendment outlawed the restrictive poll tax. President Johnson, like President Eisenhower before him, urged an amendment to include in the electorate all citizens above the age of eighteen. Meanwhile, many changes by individual states—for example, the reducing of residence requirements and the easing of absentee registration and absentee voting—have gone in the same direction. Since 1950, Alabama and South Carolina have reduced their residence requirements from two years to one; New York, to three months; Pennsylvania has reduced its requirements to ninety days; and New Jersey, to one of the lowest, forty days. All this is impressive evidence of our historic determination to make ours truly a system of majority rule.

THE MYSTERY OF THE MAJORITY

These are the changes that meet the eye and that have made the headlines. They are not so much a revolution in American political life as a fulfillment of its promise. They are not beyond the imaginings of a Jefferson, a Jackson, or a Lincoln.

But at the same time, there has taken place an unpredictable, unadvertised revolution in our political consciousness. It has been so deep, so widespread, and even so obvious, that it has gone almost unnoticed. It has been accomplished not by laws or constitutional amendments but by all the forces shaping American life—by our economy, our technology, our systems of education, and our new modes of scientific thought. It had begun by the early years of this century, but reaches a clamorous climax in our time. It could not have been imagined by a Jefferson, a Jackson, or a Lincoln. It has transformed the very meaning of political numbers, has given new content to the very notions of majority and minority. It has even undermined the very assumptions on which the system of majority rule traditionally had rested.

Majority rule rested on a democratic faith. This was a faith in the long-run prudence and wisdom of the greater number of voters. It translated into domestic politics Voltaire's assertion that "God is on the side of the big battalions." "In God we trust." Our political system, then, like others, has historically rested on belief that the right to govern derives from some higher power.

The higher mystery, in our representative government, has been embodied in the sacrament of the ballot box. There the Many become the One. On Election Day, the separate wills of millions of citizens become a single, clear "mandate." *"Vox populi, vox dei"*—the voice of the people is the voice of God—simply expresses "the divinity that doth hedge a majority."

The weaknesses and indecisions and selfishnesses of all the individual voters become purified and transformed. Behind this quasi-religious belief in the divine right of the majority, and giving it some reality in the commonsense world, was a simple fact. The majority really *was* a mystery. The single voice of the majority as it issued from thousands of ballot boxes could be heard loud and clear. But who could be sure of what it would say? Who could be sure of which particular voices had entered its resonance?

By a series of steps, now nearly forgotten, our voting system was changed to preserve, deepen, and keep sacred this mystery of the majority. Originally, most states actually did not have the secret ballot: voters stood up before neighbors and announced their preference, which was then marked on a public scoreboard. Only gradually did the secrecy of each citizen's vote come to be protected. At first, each party printed its own "ticket" (commonly a different color from that of the other parties), but spectators could still see a voter's preference by the color of his voting paper.

The campaign for the secret (or so-called "Australian") ballot began in earnest in the 1880's. What was probably our first secret-ballot law was enacted by Kentucky on February 24, 1888. Other states followed. Reformers argued that there could be no true democracy without the secret ballot. For secrecy reduced incentives to bribery and intimidation, made it impossible for corrupt politicians to be sure they were getting the votes they were willing to pay for, and so purified the voice of the majority.

The democratic paradox, which itself became an article of faith, was that majority rule really worked only so long as it could *not* be known precisely who was in the majority. This was the Mystery of the Majority. Of course, the elections themselves produced some voting statistics—on wards, congressional districts, or states—from which shrewd politicians could draw their own conclusions. But these official statistics were always wholesale and geographic. The Mystery of the Majority remained a mystery, which an enlarging and mobile electorate and a secret ballot only made more impenetrable.

VOTER SCIENCE AND
MINORITY CONSCIOUSNESS

Then there came upon the American scene a potent new force. It did more than anyone had believed possible—within the ground rules of honest elections—to dissolve the Mystery of the Majority. It was destined to transform popular thinking about elections and about the makeup of majorities and minorities and voting blocs. It would become a new weapon in the arsenal of minorities. It quickly became so familiar that its novelty and its significance were not generally noted. I will call this new political force Voter Science.

The roots of voter science went deep into the nineteenth century. Under the influence of such thinkers as Auguste Comte, Charles Darwin, Karl Marx, Herbert Spencer, and others, the belief became widespread that human society itself could become the subject of science. More than that, they even argued that a new "social" science was essential to human progress. The new social scientists assigned themselves the task of describing and predicting human behavior. Their motto was "Nothing sacred!" After Darwin had penetrated the mysteries of the creation, after Marx had offered his "laws" of the origins of property and social classes, and then, in the early twentieth century, after Freud had obtruded science into the private world of dreams and the intimacies of sex, it was inevitable that devotees of the new social sciences should make a science of the ballot box. The dimly lit salon where political "philosophers" conversed about the good society and the forms of government was displaced by the bright modern laboratory of the new political scientists. There—in the whole living, working, voting society—they counted, measured, interviewed and questionnaired in their effort to discover (in Harold Lasswell's phrase) "Who gets what, when, how."

The great development of voter science took place right here in the United States. There was no one founder, for many currents of American thought flowed into this new stream. In his classic *Public Opinion* (1922) and *The Phantom Public* (1925), Walter Lippmann began to treat the mass of voters not as an unpredictable "mob" but as a real entity with laws of its own. Significantly, the needs of American advertisers gave birth to market researchers who were the first scientific opinion pollers. Their techniques were soon applied to politics. Elmo Roper's pioneering *Fortune* poll in 1935 replaced gentlemanly conjectures and cracker-barrel hunches by scientific sampling, facts, figures, and statistics. George Gallup founded the American Institute of Public Opinion, followed by the National Opinion Research Center, and by the enterprises of Louis Harris and others.

The polls became a potent new force for the self-fulfilling political prophecy—though not without some objections. In 1935, a bill was introduced into the 74th Congress to stop the "vicious practice" of opinion polling, by prohibiting polls to use the mails. But the polls flourished. Within a decade, the pollsters became a well-organized profession, with a voluminous technical literature and annual receipts running into the millions. Despite occasional lapses—most notably in the presidential election of 1948—their margins of error generally tended to decrease. As they became more cautious, more aware of their public responsibilities, they gained the confidence of the voting public and of the candidates. Nowadays, when we talk of "the polls," we are less likely to mean the sacred ritual of the ballot box than the scientific predictions of the ubiquitous pollsters.

The techniques of statistical prediction of voting behavior were sharpened and broadened in still other ways. Enterprising voter scientists like Samuel Lubell spent months asking searching questions of individual voters, and developed new interviewing methods for depth studies of key towns and counties. Lubell's postmortem on the election of 1948, for example, did much to help pollsters discover where they had made their errors, and so helped them refine their instruments of prediction. Meanwhile, the unprecedented growth of all the social sciences, and especially of sociology, in prosperous American universities aided by newly rich foundations, provided new conceptual tools and vast new stores of facts and figures.

In the United States—"A nation of immigrants"—sociology tended to become a science of minorities. Works like Znaniecki and Thomas's five volumes on the Polish immigrant (1918–21) and Louis Wirth's book on the Jewish ghetto (1928) set a pattern for many others, like Gunnar Myrdal's monumental study of the Negro in America (1944). This sociology of minorities nourished the self-consciousness of all minorities, making each aware of its special traditions, problems, needs, powers, and opportunities.

The majority soon discovered that it really consisted of myriad minorities. The lesson of it all was contained in the quip that now 99.6 per cent of the American people were members of minority groups. And these minorities were not all ethnic. The new popular sociology explained to more and more Americans that they were themselves members of statistically definable groups, some of which they had never imagined to exist. Categories like "white-collar workers," "junior executives," "senior citizens," "urbanites," "suburbanites," and "teen-agers" became familiar. More people began to think of themselves as "consumers." And our popular sociologists have done a great deal to give a regular minority status to "Poverty-Americans."

The polls and the sociology of minorities were to domestic political strategy what Intelligence was to battlefield strategy. Voter scientists, without even intending it, became a kind of CIA for every American minority. To the Negroes, for example, who comprised only some 11 per cent of the population, they heralded a new political power. Armed with newly detailed analyses of the past Negro vote, with scientifically sampled predictions of Negro voting behavior, social attitudes, aspirations, and prejudices all over the country, Negro leaders (like other minority leaders) now had a new grasp of their voting power. Negroes now discovered that despite their disfranchisement in the South, they actually held the balance of voting power in crucial Northern cities in states with decisive blocs of electoral votes. It was such facts as these which understandably led the Washington director of the NAACP in 1951 to favor retention of the Electoral College and to oppose the direct election of the president. There was a good deal of information to support the claim that a few thousand strategically placed Negro votes actually gave John F. Kennedy his narrow victory in 1960.

ALL THE CANDIDATES IN
EVERYBODY'S LIVING ROOM

While these developments have tended to fragment the voting public, still other new forces have drawn the voting public together. Television has created a truly political audience. The clue to TV's subtle transformation of our political consciousness is that the TV audience is *unselective*.

The more revolutionary significance of the TV "Great Debates" between candidate Nixon and candidate Kennedy in 1960 (which candidate Nixon prudently refused to reenact in 1968) was not that so many people now came face-to-face with their own candidate for President. The more potent novelty was that now for the first time so many of the partisans of each candidate were forced to come face-to-face with the candidate they had not favored. By electronic magic, the political audiences of both parties were instantly combined. This was a new liberation, a new enlargement of life, that TV brought to the American voter. This widened everybody's political world. It smuggled into everybody's consciousness the personalities and images and ideas of all the major candidates. It became virtually impossible for any citizen to confine his experience of a political campaign to seeing and hearing his own pre-chosen candidate.

This was the effect not only of the Great Debates but of the very nature of television, which accentuated the tendencies which came in with radio. Formerly, political information or propaganda had come to each voter in separate, small packages (for example, in a newspaper, a magazine, or a political pamphlet). The citizen, simply by choosing his newspaper or magazines, could imprison himself in his own point of view. He could confine his reading to a Republican paper, to a Democratic paper, or even, if he chose, to the *Daily Worker*. "Other" points of view did not enter his mind uninvited; he purposely chose his news and propaganda packages because they left out those others. He was unlikely to wander by accident into a rally for the party he disliked, much less to see the faces or hear the voices of extremists or revolutionaries. Television changed all that.

Now, political information and campaign propaganda come in constantly flowing streams through the networks' broadcasting channels. The same streams flow into at least 93 per cent of American homes. Since it is impossible for the broadcaster to select his audience (repeated efforts to introduce pay TV have met little national success), the broadcaster must send out something for everybody. Now, therefore, almost everybody has to watch what anybody wants to watch. In one sense, of course, the programming is left to each TV viewer. But many words and pictures and ideas reach him before he can tune them out, and he is constantly being tempted to watch a little before deciding to change the channel.

The broadcasting flow brings all points of view into everybody's living room. People become tolerant of personalities and ideas that have some entertainment value, even if they hate the personalities and ideas and do not want to be persuaded. The whole spectrum of differing views now intrudes itself. Now, you actually have to change the channel to send the unwanted spokesman away!

TV has had a revolutionary effect also on the conspicuousness and persuasive reach of political minorities. From their point of view, the old question of "equal time" begins to be obsolete. The very nature of TV offers a new national forum for spokesmen of unpopular views. New forums, like the vastly popular interview and conversation shows of David Susskind, Johnny Carson, Irv Kupcinet, Joey Bishop, and others, give these new minorities a new voice, a vivid image, and network time they could never afford to buy. The more violent their point of view or their personality, the more apt they are to be considered "newsworthy." Zany ideas, preferably expressed by zany people, have surefire appeal. They liven up the show, raise the Neilsen ratings—and make national celebrities out of political oddballs. No view is too marginal, no political slogan too outrageous to be denied its moment on the center of the stage. The network flow brings Democratic candidates into the homes of diehard Republicans and Republican candidates into the homes of diehard Democrats, but it also brings into everybody's home both George Wallace and Eldridge Cleaver.

One obvious consequence of this nationalization of the voter audience, along with other forces, is a tendency (in Neal R. Peirce's phrase) toward the nationalization of our presidential politics. Not so long ago, presidential candidates did not even bother to campaign in the South: the Republican candidate found it useless, and the Democratic candidate found it unnecessary. Eight Southern states had never gone to a Republican candidate for President between 1876 and 1928; six other states had almost always gone Republican. But times have changed. In 1968, candidate Nixon found it important to campaign in the South. Candidate Humphrey's failure to carry any state east of Texas and south of West Virginia was crucial in putting together the narrow Republican victory. And it showed that now there are virtually no safe "one-party" states. Since the first election of Franklin Delano Roosevelt, no state has failed to vary its party allegiance. Even Vermont went Democratic in 1964; and even in North Carolina (with its Republican congressmen) and in Arkansas (with a Republican governor), we have begun to see signs of the newly nationalized politics. It is significant, too, that the most populous states—New York, California, Pennsylvania, Illinois, and Ohio—are among the most variable in their presidential voting allegiance and have tended to give the narrowest margins to the winners.

NEW ANSWERS FOR NEW QUESTIONS

New forces, then, shape the consciousness of our voters. The components of the numerical majority are no longer shrouded in mystery. Voter science, reenforced by a new and newly popular sociology, has created newly self-conscious minorities, armed with new techniques and with a new sense of their voting power. Everywhere-minorities cover the country. For the first time, they know precisely who they are, precisely where they are, what they can demand, and what they can deliver. The campaign audience, too, has been transformed—not only enlarged, but essentially changed. Campaigning, once it has moved into the flowing TV channels, tends more and more to preach to the unconverted. The eyes of the partisan citizen are opened, he is liberated from himself. And lest he be tempted to believe in a cozy two-party world, he is confronted willy-nilly by unsavory extremists who acquire a new national conspicuousness as they walk right into everybody's living room in the costumes of entertainers. The old, safe, two-party world, with its neat geographic blocs, is no longer with us. We still have a system of two-party politics, but American voters no longer live in the old two-party world.

Perhaps this discord between the new realities of our political thinking and feeling and learning and our time-honored election system helps explain why so much recent "political" activity has been extra-political. Is it surprising that Americans see a new unreality in our political and electoral system and come to find it less and less "representative"? The old clichés of majority rule will no longer serve. What we are getting is old answers to old questions. We hear new support for old movements to reform our election system. Direct election of the President by popular vote (in place of the old Electoral College), which was proposed in Congress as early as 1816, is more widely favored today than ever before. The uncertainties of the 1968 election, and the narrowness with which a resort to the House of Representatives was avoided, reenforced demands to change the ways of counting presidential votes and to provide new insurance against deadlock. The next few years will probably see a constitutional amendment reducing the presidential voting age to eighteen. Residence requirements for presidential voting will be further reduced or abolished. We hear demands for a single national presidential primary to pick party candidates. We hear proposals to revise the procedures of the national party conventions and to change their time of meeting.

These and other reforms aim, for the most part, to make our presidential election a more accurate expression of the will of the majority. Many of them are desirable. Some are urgent.

But new powers are abroad in the land—in the streets, in the factories, in the universities, on our television channels, and even in our churches—nearly everywhere perhaps except in our national political system. Is it too much to expect our representative system to provide voters at the polls in a presidential year an opportunity to express their honest disagreement over the major questions of national policy? For example, to vote their opposition to the war in Vietnam or their criticisms of its conduct? Or must they be left to explode in myriad extra-political forms?

For the majority is no longer a mystery. The new minorities are plainer than ever to see and almost impossible to avoid hearing. Without ever having intended it, we have acquired a national politics and become a new democracy of minorities. The flexibility and adaptability of our system are being tested. Can it respond to a new world of voter science and electronic magic?

If our political life is to stay indoors—if more and more of our political life is not to move from the ballot box and the legislative hall into the street or onto the barricades—we must find new political voices for these new minorities, legitimate political voices, numerically registered and nationally audible.

VII

THE NEW

BARBARIANS:

 ## THE DECLINE

OF RADICALISM

For centuries, men here have been discovering new ways in which the happiness and prosperity of each individual revolves around that of the community. Now suddenly we are witnessing the explosive rebellion of small groups, who reject the American past, deny their relation to the community, and in a spiritual Ptolemaism insist that the U.S.A. must revolve around each of them. This atavism, this New Barbarism, cannot last, if the nation is to survive.

Because the New Barbarians seek the kudos of old labels —"Non-violence," "Pacifism," "Leftism," "Radicalism," etc.—we too readily assume that they really are just another expression of "good old American individualism," of "healthy dissent," of the red-blooded rambunctious spirit which has kept this country alive and kicking.

Nothing could be further from the truth. We are now seeing something new under the American sun. And we will be in still deeper trouble if we do not recognize what has really happened. The New Barbarism is not simply another ex-

pression of American vitality. It is not simply another expression of the utopianism of youth. On the contrary. What
it expresses, in tornado-potence, is a new view of America
and of the world. It expresses a new notion of how the world
should be grasped.

WHAT IS RADICALISM?

The Depression Decade beginning in 1929 saw in the
United States a host of radicalisms, perhaps more numerous
and more influential than at any earlier period of our history. Many of these were left-wing movements, which included large numbers of our academics, intellectuals, and
men of public conscience, who became members or fellow
travelers of groups dominated by Marxist ideas. They favored a reconstruction of American life on a base of socialism or communism. Some of them had a great deal to do
with promoting a new and wider American labor movement,
with helping F.D.R. popularize the need for a welfare state,
and with persuading Americans to join the war to stop Hitler.
Although they fenced in American social scientists by new
orthodoxies, they did have a generally tonic effect on American society. However misguided were many of the policies
they advocated, these radicals did help awaken and sensitize
the American conscience. They confronted Americans with
some facts of life which had been swept under the rug.

That was radicalism. And those of us who were part of it
can attest to some of its features. It was radicalism in the
familiar and traditional sense of the word. The word "radical" does, of course, come from the Latin *radix,* meaning
"root," and a radical, then, is a person trying to go to the
root of matters.

Of course those radicals never were quite respectable.
Their message was that things were not what they seemed,

which inevitably makes respectable people uncomfortable. But we would be mistaken if we assumed, as many do nowadays, that a radical is anybody who makes lots of other people uncomfortable.

What makes a radical radical is not *that* he discomfits others but *how* he does it. A drunk is not a radical, neither is a psychotic, though both can make us quite uncomfortable. Nor does mere rudeness or violence make a person a radical, though a rude or violent man can make everybody around him quite miserable. Nor is a man who is unjustly treated and resents it necessarily a radical. Caryl Chessman may not have been guilty as charged—yet that did not make him a radical.

The most vocal and most violent disrupters of American society today are not radicals at all, but a new species of barbarian. In the ancient world, "barbarian" was a synonym for foreigner, and meant an alien who came from some far-off savage land. He himself was "barbarous," wild, and uncivilized. He was a menace not because he wanted to reform or reshape the society he invaded but because he did not understand or value that society, and he aimed to destroy it.

The New Barbarians in America today come not from without, but from within. While they are not numerous anywhere—comprising perhaps less than 2 per cent of our two hundred million Americans—they pose a special threat precisely because they are diffuse, wild, and disorganized. They have no one or two headquarters to be surveyed, no one or two philosophies to be combated. But they are no less rude, wild, and uncivilized than if they had come from the land of the Visigoths or the Vandals. The fact that they come from within—and are somehow a product of—our society makes them peculiarly terrifying, but it does not make them any the less barbarians.

We must not be deceived by our own hypersensitive liberal consciences, nor by the familiar, respected labels under which the New Barbarians like to travel. If American civilization is to survive, if we are to resist and defeat the New Barbarism, we must see it for what it is. Most important, we must see that in America the New Barbarism is something really new.

A first step in this direction is to cease to confuse the New Barbarians with the members of other, intellectually respectable groups which can and must claim tolerance in a free society. The New Barbarians are not radicals. This will be obvious if we recall the characteristics of the radicalisms that in one form or another have discomfited and awakened generations of Americans.

Radicalism in the United States has had several distinctive and interrelated characteristics:

1. *Radicalism Is a Search for Meaning.* The search for meaning is the search for significance, for what else something connotes. The socialist, for example, denies that the capitalist system of production and distribution makes sense; he wants to reorganize it to produce a new meaning in the institutions of property and in the economy of the whole society. The religious pacifist, if he is a Christian, seeks the meaning of society in the Christian vision of peace and the brotherhood of man. When the true radical criticizes society he demands that the society justify itself according to some new measure of meaning.

2. *Radicalism Has a Specific Content.* The radical is distinguished from the man who simply has a bad digestion by the fact that the radical's belief has some solid subject matter, while the other man is merely dyspeptic. A stomach ache or sheer anger or irritability cannot be the substance of radicalism. Thus, while a man can be ill-natured or irritable in general, he cannot be a radical in general. Every radicalism

is a way of asserting *what* are the roots. Radicalism, therefore, involves affirmation. It is distinguished from conserva-
tism precisely in that the conservative can be loose and
vague about his affirmation. The conservative is in fact always tempted to let his affirmation become mere compla-
cency. But the true radical cannot refuse to affirm, and to be
specific, although of course he may be utopian. The radical
must affirm that *this* is more fundamental than that. One
great service of the radical, then, is that by his experimental
definitions he puts the conservative on the defensive and
makes him discover, decide, and define what is really worth
preserving. The radical does this by the specificity (sometimes also by the rashness) of his affirmation—of the dicta-
torship of the proletariat, of the Kingdom of God on earth,
or of whatever else.

3. *Radicalism Is an Affirmation of Community.* It affirms
that we all share the same root problems, that we are all in
the same boat, though the radical may see the boat very
differently than do others. For example, if he is a pacifist
radical he insists that the whole society bears the blame for
even a single man killed in war; if he is an anarchist radical
he insists that the whole society bears the blame for the in-
justice of property and the violence of government. Radicalism, then, involves a commitment to the interdependence of
men, and to the sharing of their concerns, which the radical
feels with an especially urgent, personal intensity.

These are only general characteristics. Of course, there
are borderline cases. We might be uncertain whether Henry
George's Single Taxers or Tom Watson's Populists were real
radicals. But a full-fledged radicalism, of the kind which can
serve and has served as a tonic to the whole society, does
have at least the three characteristics I have mentioned.
There have been many such radicalisms in American History—from the Antinomians of Massachusetts Bay, through

the Quakers of Pennsylvania, the Abolitionists, and the Mormons down to the Jehovah's Witnesses and the Communists in our own day. But the most prominent, the most vocal, the most threatening, and the most characteristic disruptive movements in the United States within the last few years do not belong in this tradition. Whatever they or their uncritical observers may say to the contrary, they are not radicalisms. They do not exhibit the characteristics I have listed.

FROM THE QUEST FOR MEANING
TO THE QUEST FOR POWER

It is characteristic of the Student Power and the Black Power "movements" that in them the quest for meaning has been displaced by the quest for power. Among students, the Bull Session tends to be displaced by the Strategy Session. The "discussions" of activist students are not explorations of the great questions that have troubled civilized men as they come to manhood, since the days of the Old Testament and of Ancient Greece. They are not concerned with whether there is a God, with what is the true nature of art, or of civilization, or of morals. The Student Power Barbarians and the Black Power Barbarians pose not questions but answers. Or, as one of their recent slogans says: "Happiness Is Student Power." Their answer to everything is uncharmingly simple: Power. And to the more difficult questions their answer is: More Power.

These New Barbarians offer no content, no ideology, hardly even a jargon. While dissident students thirty-five years ago spoke an esoteric Marxist lingo, and debated "dialectical materialism," "the transformation of quantity into quality," etc., etc., the dissident students and Black Powerites today scream four-letter obscenities and expletives. While the radicals explored an intricate ideology in the heavy volumes of Marx, the cumbersome paragraphs of Lenin, and the elaborate reinterpretations of Stalin and Trotsky, today's power-seekers are more than satisfied by the hate slogans of Mao Tse-tung, Che Guevara, or Malcolm X. They find nothing so enchanting as the sound of their own voices, and their bibliography consists mainly of the products of their own mimeographing. They seem to think they can be radicals without portfolio. If they call themselves "anarchists" they have not bothered to read their Thoreau or Proudhon, Bakunin or Tolstoy. If they call themselves "leftists" they have not bothered to read Marx or Engels, Lenin or Trotsky. If they call themselves Black Power Nationalists, they mistake the rattle of ancient chains for the sound of facts and ideas.

Having nothing to say, the New Barbarians cannot interest others by *what* they say. Therefore, they must try to shock by how they say it. Traditionally, radicals have addressed their society with a question mark, but the new frustrates' favorite punctuation is the exclamation point. Having no new facts or ideas to offer, they strain at novelty with their latrine words. The Black Powerites, whose whole program is their own power, must wrap up their emptiness in vulgarisms and expletives. For racism is the perfect example of a dogma without content.

The appeal to violence and "direct action" as if they were ends rather than means is eloquent testimony of the New Barbarians' lack of subject matter. An act of violence may express hate or anger, but it communicates nothing precise or substantial. Throwing a rock, like hurling an epithet, proclaims that the thrower has given up trying to say anything.

These Student Powerites and Black Powerites are not

egalitarians seeking a just community; they are *egolitarians,* preening the egoism of the isolationist self. Students seek power for "students," Negroes seek power for "blacks"— and let the community take the hindmost! Unlike the radicalisms which affirm community and are preoccupied or obsessed by its problems, the Student Power and Black Power movements deny any substantial community—even among their own "members." A novel feature of S.N.C.C. and S.D.S., too little noted, is the fact that they are, strictly speaking, "non-membership" organizations. Members do not carry cards, membership lists are said not to exist. A person does not "join" as a result of long and solemn deliberation, he is not trained and tested (as was the case in the Thirties with candidates for membership in the Communist Party). Instead the New Barbarian simply affiliates, and stays with the group as long as it pleases him. "I'm with you today, baby, but who knows where I'll be tomorrow?" A desperate infant-instantism reveals the uncertainty and vagrancy of these affiliations. The leader better act this afternoon, for maybe they won't be with him tomorrow morning!

All these unradical characteristics of the New Barbarians express a spiritual cataclysm. This is what I mean by the Ptolemaic Revolution: a movement from the community-centered to the self-centered. While radicals see themselves and everything else revolving around the community and its idealized needs, each of these new frustrates tries to make the world revolve around himself. The depth and significance of this shift in focus have remained unnoticed. It has been the harder to grasp because it is in the nature of the New Barbarism that it should lack philosophers. Being closer to a dyspepsia than to an ideology, the New Barbarism has tried to generalize its stomach aches but it has been unable to cast them into a philosophy. It is much easier, therefore, to describe the direction in which the chaotic groups comprising the New Barbarism are moving than to fix the precise position where they stand.

FROM EXPERIENCE TO SENSATION

The New Barbarism, in a word, is the social expression of a movement from Experience to Sensation. Experience, the dictionary tells us, means *actual observation of or practical acquaintance with facts or events; knowledge resulting from this.* A person's experience is what he has lived through. Generally speaking, experience is (a) cumulative, and (b) communicable. People add up their experiences to become wiser and more knowledgeable. We can learn from our own experience and, most important, we can learn from other people's experiences. Our publicly shared experience is history. Experience is distinguished, then, by the very fact that it can be shared. When we have an experience, we enter into the continuum of a society. But the dramatic shift now is away from Experience and toward Sensation.

Sensation is personal, private, confined, and incommunicable. Our sensations (hearing, seeing, touching, tasting, and smelling) are what we receive. Or, as the dictionary says, sensation is *consciousness of perceiving or seeming to perceive some state or affection of one's body or its parts or senses of one's mind or its emotions; the contents of such consciousness.* If an experience were totally incommunicable, if I could not describe it to anyone else, if I could not share it, it would not really be an experience. It would simply be a sensation, a message which came to me and to me alone. Sensations, from their very nature, then, are intimate and ineffable. Experience takes us out of ourselves, sensation affirms and emphasizes the self.

What history is to the person in quest of experience, a "happening" is to the person in quest of sensation. For a "happening" is something totally discrete. It adds to our sensations without increasing our experience.

Experience and Sensation, then, express attitudes to the world as opposite as the poles. The experience-oriented young person suffers Weltschmerz—the discovery of the pain and suffering that are his portion of the world. The sensation-oriented suffers an "identity crisis": he is concerned mostly about defining the boundaries of that bundle of private messages which is himself. The experience-oriented seeks, and finds, continuity, and emphasizes what is shared and what is communicable. The sensation-oriented seeks the instantaneous, the egocentric, the inexpressible. The accumulation of *experience* produces the *expert*. Its cumulative product is expertise—competence, the ability to handle situations by knowing what is tried and familiar about them. And the name for accumulated experience is knowledge.

While sensations can be more or less intense, they are not cumulative. A set of simultaneous, intense, and melodramatic sensations is not instructive, but it is shocking: we say it is sensational. Experience is additive, it can be organized, classified, and rearranged; sensation is miscellaneous, random, and incapable of being generalized.

Everywhere in the United States nowadays—and not only among the New Barbarians—we see a desperate quest for sensation and a growing tendency to value sensation more than experience. We note this in what people seek, in what they find, in what they make, and in what they like to watch. We note a tendency in painting to produce works which do not appeal to a common, shareable fund of experience, but which, instead, set off each viewer on his own private path of sensation. In the theatre and in movies which lack a clear and intelligible story line, the spectators are offered sensations from which each is expected to make his own private inward adventure.

An example of the current quest for the indescribable, the ineffable, the transcendent—aiming to maximize sensation rather than experience—is the vogue for LSD and for other so-called "consciousness-expanding" drugs. Precisely speaking, they aim to expand not experience but *consciousness*. They aim somehow to increase the intensity and widen the range of the vivid, idiosyncratic self.

The special appeal of an LSD "trip" is that it leads to the ineffable: what one person gets is as different as possible from what is obtained by another. And it is all quite individual and quite unpredictable. "Instead of a communion," one psychologist explains, "it [the LSD state] is a withdrawal into oneself. The *religio* (binding together) is not visible here." This is how Richard Alpert, an archbishop of LSD, explains the sensations under the drug:

" 'Nowhere' is Sidney's prediction of where the psycho-chemical (r)evolution is taking the 'young people' who are exploring inner space. I prefer to read that word as NowHere, and fervently hope he is right—that LSD is bringing man back 'to his senses.' . . . Do not be confused! The issue is not LSD. . . . Your control and access to your own brain is at stake."

LSD sensations, Alpert insists, are "eyewitness reports of what is, essentially, a private experience." "It was," in the words of a girl who had just been on an LSD trip, "like a shower on the inside."

The search for sensation is a search for some way of reminding oneself that one is alive—but without becoming entangled with others or with a community. "I have never felt so intense, alive, such a sense of well-being. . . . I have chosen to be outside of society after having been very much inside. . . . My plans are unstructured in regards to anything but the immediate future. I believe in freedom, and must take the jump, I must take the chance of action." This is not the report of an LSD trip, but the explanation by a young white student of his sensations on joining S.N.C.C. The vocabulary of the Student Power movement reveals the same desperate quest for sensation.

THE APATHETES

"Direct Action" is the name for spasmodic acts of self-affirmation. It is a way of making the senses scream. It matters not whether the "Direct Action" has a purpose, much less whether it can attain any purpose, since it gives satisfaction enough by intensifying the Direct Actor's sense of being alive and separate from others. "Direct Action" is to politics what the Frug or the Jerk is to the dance. It identifies and explodes the self without attaching the self to groups or to individuals outside. And now the "New Left" has become the LSD of the intellectuals.

The man who is pathologically Experience-oriented will be timid, haunted by respectability. His motto is apt to be that posted over the desk of an English civil servant: "Never do anything for the first time!" On the other hand, the man pathologically obsessed by Sensation makes his motto: "Do everything only for the first time!"

All about us, and especially in the Student Power and Black Power movements of recent years, we see the pathology of the sensation-oriented. Contrary to popular belief and contrary to the legends which they would like to spread about themselves, they are not troubled by any excessive concern for others. Their feelings cannot accurately be described as a concern, and it is surely not for others. Their ailment might best be called *apathy*. For apathy is a feeling apart from others and, as the dictionary reminds us, *an indolence of mind*. The Direct Actionists, as President W. Allen Wallis of the University of Rochester has explained, "are the students who are truly apathetic." They do not care enough about the problems of their society to burn the midnight oil over them. Impatient to sate their egos with the sensations of "Direct Action," they are too indolent intellectually to do the hard work of exploring the problems to which they pretend a concern. Theirs is the egoism, the personal chauvinism of the isolationist self. Their "Direct Action" slogan means nothing but "Myself, Right or Wrong!"

These people I would call the *Apathetes*. Just as the Aesthetes of some decades ago believed in "Art for Art's Sake," so the Apathetes believe in "Me for My Own Sake." They try to make a virtue of their indolence of mind (by calling it "Direct Action") and they exult in their feeling-apartness (by calling it "Power"). Thus these Apathetes are at the opposite pole from the radicals of the past.

They abandon the quest for meaning, for fear it might entangle their thoughts and feelings with those of others, and they plunge into "Direct Action" for fear that second thoughts might deny them this satisfaction to their ego. Theirs is a mindless, obsessive quest for power. But they give up the very idea of man's need for quest. Instead they seek explosive affirmations of the self.

They deny the existence of subject matter, by denying the need for experience. How natural, then, that Youth should lord it over Age! For in youth, they say, the senses are most sensitive and most attuned. The accumulated experience of books or of teachers becomes absurdly irrelevant. There is no Knowledge, but only Sensation, and Power is its Handmaiden!

TOWARD THE AGE OF
INSTANT EVERYTHING

They deny the existence of time, since Sensation is instantaneous and not cumulative. They herald the age of Instant Everything. Since time can do nothing but accumulate experience and dull the senses, experience is said to be nothing but the debris which stifles our sensations. There must be no frustration. Every program must be instantaneous, every demand must be an ultimatum.

This movement from Experience to Sensation accelerates every day. Each little victory for Student Power or Black Power—or any other kind of Power—is a victory for the New Barbarism. Appropriately, the New Barbarism makes its first sallies and has its greatest initial successes against the universities, which are the repositories of Experience, and in the cause of Racism, which—Black or Aryan—is the emptiness to end all emptinesses.

ACKNOWLEDGMENTS

This book was suggested by my wife, Ruth F. Boorstin, who, as usual, has been my principal editor. I take special satisfaction in offering it to the memory of two people who did much to cheer both of us on the search of which the book is a part. The discrimination and judgment of my friend Jess Stein, Vice-President of Random House, have been invaluable. Once again, Leonore C. Hauck of Random House has helped make this book attractive. My research assistants in recent years, and especially Stanley Schultz, Peter Marzio, and Perry Duis, have helped in innumerable ways.

The University of Chicago has continued to provide me a free and stimulating environment.

Two of these chapters, "From Charity to Philanthropy" and "The Perils of Indwelling Law," have not been published before. The others have appeared, in slightly different form, in various publications. I wish to thank their editors and publishers for permission to reprint. "The Rise of the Average Man" appeared as an introduction to the reissue of the

Statistical Abstract of the United States under the title *The U.S. Book of Facts, Statistics & Information, for 1967* (Washington Square Press, 1966). "Welcome to the Consumption Community" appeared in *Fortune,* September 1, 1967, Vol. LXXVI, No. 3, at pp. 118–120, 131–38. "From Charity to Philanthropy," originally a lecture delivered at the University of Chicago on October 15, 1962, was part of the celebration of the one hundredth anniversary of the birth of Julius Rosenwald. "The Perils of Indwelling Law" was a paper offered at the Conference on Law and the Humanities, under the auspices of the American Council of Learned Societies in New York City, on May 13, 1961. "Dissent, Dissension, and the News" was a talk to the annual meeting of The Associated Press Managing Editors' Association in Chicago on October 13, 1967, and was later circulated by the Associated Press. "The End of Our Two-Party World" appeared in *Look,* August 20, 1968, Vol. 32, No. 17, at pp. 37–43. "The New Barbarians" appeared in the thirty-fifth anniversary issue of *Esquire,* October, 1968, Vol. LXX, No. 4, at pp. 159–62, 260–63.

Readers of *The Americans: The Colonial Experience* and *The Americans: The National Experience* (Random House; Vintage Books) will notice that in some of these chapters I have carried further and applied in other areas certain ideas found there. Some of the suggestions in the present volume will be further explored in the third volume of *The Americans.*

INDEX

[Index]

DANIEL J. BOORSTIN, the Preston & Sterling Morton Distinguished Service Professor of American History at the University of Chicago, is widely known for his fresh interpretations of the American past, which he uses to illuminate the American present. He is now the Director of The National Museum of History and Technology.

Born in Georgia and raised in Oklahoma, he received his undergraduate degree from Harvard and his doctor's degree from Yale. As a Rhodes Scholar at Oxford he won that university's highest academic honor, a "double first," and was admitted as a barrister-at-law of the Inner Temple, London. He has lectured around the world, and has held professorships at the Sorbonne and at Cambridge University.

Dr. Boorstin is the author of numerous books, including *The Genius of American Politics* and *The Image.* He is perhaps best known for his original and influential reinterpretation of American history, *The Americans,* the first volume of which (*The Americans: The Colonial Experience*) was awarded the Bancroft Prize and the second volume of which (*The Americans: The National Experience*) was awarded the Francis Parkman Prize. He is currently at work on the final volume of the trilogy. And he has offered a lively new view of American history for young readers in his *Landmark History of the American People.*